ARCHBISHOP ROMERO: MARTYR OF SALVADOR

ARCHBISHOP ROMERO: MARTYR OF SALVADOR

PLÁCIDO ERDOZAÍN

Foreword by Jorge Lara-Braud

Translated by John McFadden and Ruth Warner

ORBIS BOOKS
Maryknoll, New York 10545

Third Printing, April 1984

The Catholic Foreign Mission Society of America (Maryknoll) recruits and trains people for overseas missionary service. Through Orbis Books Maryknoll aims to foster the international dialogue that is essential to mission. The books published, however, reflect the opinions of their authors and are not meant to represent the official position of the society.

Photo Credits:
Octavio Durán: pp. xxvi, 20, 40, 41, 56, 57, 72
National Catholic Reporter: pp. xxiv, 101
Foto Estudio Flores, San Salvador: p. 87 bottom
Foto Sol, San Salvador: p. 88 top
Estudio Canossa, San Salvador: p. 88 bottom
Maryknoll Sisters: p. 99

Photo Editor: Catherine Costello

Originally published as *Monseñor Romero: Mártir de la Iglesia Popular,* copyright © 1980 by Departamento Ecuménico de Investigaciones (Apdo. 339, S. Pedro Montes de Oca, San José, Costa Rica) and Editorial Universitaria Centroamericana (EDUCA).

This English translation, including revisions, copyright © 1981 by Orbis Books, Maryknoll, NY 10545

Manufactured in the United States of America

To the Memories of

Juan Chacón, General Secretary of the BPR
Ita Ford, Maryknoll missioner
Maura Clarke, Maryknoll missioner
Dorothy Kazel, Ursuline missioner
Jean Donovan, lay missioner, Cleveland Diocese
Marcial Serrano, Pastor of Olocuita parish
Ernesto Abrego, priest returning to El Salvador

All killed between November 27 and December 2, 1980,
because they were committed, practicing Christians
in a country where this has become a crime.

They were the latest part of the continuing story told
in this book.

Contents

Foreword, by Jorge Lara-Braud   ix
Translators' Preface   xxi
Acronyms   xxv

I. Elements of a Portrait   *1*

The Context   2
Milestones in the Bishop's Life   4
February 8, 1977—Meeting in Santa Lucía   5
February 13, 1977—Demonstration in Apopa   9
February 28, 1977—Massacre in Plaza Libertad   10
March 12, 1977—Rutilio Grande, Martyr   13
April 1977—First Pastoral Letter   17
May 11, 1977—Alfonso Navarro, Martyr   18

II. Education of a Bishop   *21*

The Chancery Coffee Lounge   22
May 19, 1977—Martyrdom of Aguilares   23
June 1977—Learning from the People   26
July 1, 1977—Presidential Inauguration, Episcopal
    Abstention   30
August 1977—Second Pastoral Letter   30
The Bishop's Sunday Sermons   32
An Auxiliary Bishop   34
1978—Third Pastoral Letter   36

III. Crossfire   42

November 28, 1978—Ernesto Barrera, Guerrilla-
   Priest   43
The Bishop and the Labor Movement   49
January 20, 1979—Octavio Ortiz, Martyr   52
Bishop Romero in Puebla   54

IV. Crisis and Popular Mobilization   58

June 1979—Nicaragua Explodes   60
June 20, 1979—Rafael Palacios, Martyr   60
August 4, 1979—Alirio Napoleón Macías, Martyr   62
August 1979—Fourth Pastoral Letter   64
The People Rebuffed Again   66
The Juntas and the Crisis in the Salvadoran Church   68

V. The Path to Calvary   73

Preparing to Die   75
February 17,1980—Letter to President Carter   77
Aftermath   82
October 7, 1980—Manuel Reyes, Martyr   84

Appendix   89

Statement of the Bishops at Bishop Romero's
   Funeral   89
Communiqué of the Priests, Nuns, and Brothers of the
   Archdiocese of San Salvador   92
Press Release of the Bishop Oscar Arnulfo Romero
   National Coordinating Committee of the People's
   Church   95

Foreword

Saints and martyrs belong to the church universal, and the place of their sojourn inevitably attains the status of a shrine in the worldwide memory of fellow Christians. So it is with Oscar Arnulfo Romero of San Salvador.

Oral biographies of him abounded even before March 24, 1980, the day of his martyrdom. But it was fitting that the first one set to writing should emerge from one of the priests closest to him, who writes a frankly partisan biography. Plácido and his companions were not among the Archbishop's first admirers, and he knew it. On one occasion he told them he was expected to destroy them. Their mutual conversion to friendship is certainly no romance. The struggle and reconciliation between a conservative bishop and a cadre of radical priests is itself a parable of the larger struggle in Latin America's Roman Catholic church between pre-Vatican II traditionalists and post-Medellín liberationists.

As a Presbyterian layman, I might be seen as an intruder in these matters. But I, too, dare claim Archbishop Romero as a friend, mentor, and model. In case it might be forgotten, he was a genuine ecumenist. Few things gave him greater pleasure than to welcome representatives from other Christian churches.

I met him in June of 1977, four months after he became Archbishop of San Salvador. Father Rutilio Grande had been murdered in March and Father Alfonso Navarro in May. My organization at the time, the National Council of Churches of Christ in the U.S.A., together with the World Council of Churches, sent Dr. Thomas J. Liggett and me to express the concern of both bodies over the rapidly intensifying persecution of the Salvadoran church.

"Monseñor," as I learned everyone called the Archbishop, told us he was happy and honored to meet us. I made a mental note.

He seemed shy and distracted, even a bit intimidated. Was this little man, dressed as a country priest, the controversial firebrand we had heard so much about?

After additional pleasantries, he quickly ushered us into a large meeting room where the recently formed Emergency Committee had gathered. It was made up of diocesan and Jesuit priests, members of religious orders, lay men and women, the auxiliary bishop, Arturo Rivera y Damas, and our compatriot Tom Quigley from the U.S. Catholic Conference, who by previous agreement had arrived in time to join us.

A priest was presiding. Monseñor suddenly blended into the crowd and for a moment was indistinguishable. We quickly saw his penchant for democratic meetings; he deferred to others. He appeared not even to be one among equals. He was just one among others. The presiding priest, after introducing himself, tactfully inquired as to the reason for our visit. Now it was our turn to look shy and intimidated. We were in the presence of self-assured, battle-tested, upbeat Christians with an urgency appropriate to critical times.

In essence we said we were concerned and wished to know if we could be of help. "Yes," the priest said. "You can use your ecumenical media to let the world know what we're up against." He and others, with not a trace of self-pity, gave us then a somber summary: threats on their lives, murders of two priests and of several lay leaders, expulsion of colleagues from the country, attacks on Monseñor and his archdiocese as subversives, and recent tortures. No one had to point to the two tortured ones present. A face misshapen and an arm bent out of shape were recognizable enough.

"But why?" I asked emotionally. "Let Monseñor speak," a voice suggested. He came around the table and lightly rested his hand on my shoulder. "Doctor" (he never could get used to calling me Jorge), "our persecutors are confused. They are not yet used to seeing the face of a church converted to the poor. To raise the question of their rights is to call in question the whole established order. That is why they have no other category for us but that of subversives. And they treat us in the only way they know how:

with violent words and violent actions. But we are not giving up our position or our hope for their conversion." Another mental note: "conversion" was a key term in this gentle bishop's vocabulary.

The somberness was broken by the serving of sandwiches and soft drinks. The blessing for refreshments included the foreigners as well. In groups of four or five we carried on further conversations. Shortly thereafter, Monseñor said he had a question for the guests. This time he was decisive and a bit impish. The issue was whether we thought it wise that he should break an immemorial tradition. The man made president-elect by a gross electoral fraud, Col. Carlos Humberto Romero (no relation), had offered Monseñor a hands-off policy by the government in the conduct of church affairs if the prelate kept the unbroken tradition of invoking God's blessing upon the presidential inauguration a few days later. We looked at one another, not knowing whether we were being set up or if the query were in earnest. I guessed it was both. After each of us begged off, he pressed the question more insistently.

I searched for a parallel in my mind and came up with the closest I could remember. "Monseñor," I stammered, "Cardinal Silva, soon after the Pinochet coup, was called upon to celebrate the traditional Te Deum on Chilean Independence Day. He knew the new junta in all its military splendor would be facing him from the cathedral's first row. He took the risk for the sake of peace, and it boomeranged on him and the church. What the people heard on radio and saw on television was a blessing on the barbarians—the last thing from an act of peacemaking. Cardinal Silva, I am sure, regrets the error to this day."

"So you are telling me I should not appear at the inauguration?"

"No, Monseñor, I wouldn't dare instruct you on something so far-reaching for you, while we return safely to the States."

Then with a big grin, like a child hugely pleased at getting his way, he reassured me. "It's OK that you are saying I shouldn't. You are in good company. That's what all of these, my vigilantes, have told me in no uncertain terms." A roar of laughter went up. I was struck by the reversal of roles. We who had come to console would go away consoled by these confident, converted Christians daily having to face defamation, exile, torture, or death.

The meeting was over. Monseñor, now thoroughly at ease, escorted us to our automobile, not without begging us to carry his prayers to our families, colleagues, and organizations, and encouraging us to keep these exchanges as frequent as possible.

A week later, back home reading a tiny notice in the back pages of the *New York Times*, I beamed. According to the story the significant feature of the Salvadoran presidential inauguration was the conspicuous absence of Monseñor Romero, who according to the *Times* had deliberately boycotted the event. But I also shuddered. The rebuff certainly would not go unpunished.

It was not until a year and a half later that I was to see Monseñor again. Meanwhile we exchanged a few letters, and I became an avid researcher of everything having to do with him and the continuing persecution of his church. I joined Salvadoran solidarity committees, wrote letters to the Organization of American States, to Congress, to the State Department, and to anyone else who might listen to one more protest against the brutality unleashed against the Salvadoran church. Being a frequent speaker at church gatherings, regardless of the subject matter announced I made room for a plea to save El Salvador from the barbarians.

Monseñor was aware of my own "conversion" to his cause. He invited me to share with him the week of Prayer for Christian Unity (January 18–25, 1979). The death of Pope John Paul I had shifted the date of the Latin American Bishops' conference in Puebla, which meant he would leave for Mexico a day or two after my arrival. In any event, six evening ecumenical liturgies had been planned, alternating between a Protestant and Catholic place of worship. The first, at Emmanuel Baptist, was packed when I arrived as the guest preacher, scarcely an hour after my arrival from New York. The host pastor, Carlos Sánchez, was making a heartrending announcement just as I joined him next to the pulpit.

He was sharing a still garbled report broadcast over radio and sweeping through the barrios of San Salvador. That morning at dawn with a tank and a jeep a detachment of the National Guard had invaded the El Despertar Catholic conference center in a blaze of machinegun fire to raid what they thought or claimed to know was a training session for urban guerrillas. Killed were Father Octavio Ortiz Luna and four youngsters, who together with forty other retreatants were attending a weekend Christian initiation retreat. People broke into a combination of sobs, prayers, and shrieks of anger. I was amazed that they composed themselves quickly enough to plead that the service go on. I preached the way Monseñor had taught me, with an open Bible, and a message from God's Word of comfort and indignation, of renewed conversion to Christ's Kingdom and a prophetic denunciation against the assassins, but also a plea to God for their forgiveness. It was unbelievable. The mourners were capable of interrupting with repeated applause and cries of "Bendito sea Dios!" How well, I thought to myself, they all, Protestants and Catholics, had learned to attune themselves to the style and content of Monseñor's preaching, which they heard every Sunday over YSAX, the Catholic radio station.

Word came to us that Monseñor was expecting us at the cathedral, where the coffins had begun to arrive. He met me at a side entrance. He looked ashen but determined. He embraced me while saying, "Doctor, please say what's in your heart tonight, and tomorrow come early so you can speak at Mass. All churches will be closed. There will be a single Mass. We'll use Plaza Barrios" (the National Square, one side of which is occupied by the cathedral).

The next day, Sunday, when we arrived at the cathedral half an hour before Mass, the square was filled by no fewer than fifty thousand. The five coffins, all open, lay at the foot of the stairs leading to the cathedral's main entrance. At eight o'clock from an altar at the top of the steps the Mass began with cheerful chants and sober readings from the lectionary. At the appropriate time, Monseñor introduced me as a messenger of Christian unity speaking on behalf of the National Council of Churches in New York and the World Council of Churches in Geneva.

I was greeted with warm applause. Mine was a mini-homily, which I concluded by petitioning the Salvadoran church to forgive us, Christians of the United States, for allowing the power of our nation to reward oppressors and to manufacture more poor people. The mini-homily had been punctuated with hearty clapping, and the plea for forgiveness was followed by wave after wave of applause.

It was Monseñor's turn. Deeply moved, he thanked me on behalf of his flock for helping make real at such a solemn moment the reality of Christian unity beyond national boundaries. His homily lasted more than an hour, and it was often stopped by sustained applause. I watched him closely. He never faltered. His voice never broke. His courage kept growing. His hope kept emerging and re-emerging as he sounded the theme of living in the power of the resurrection. To the killers he announced both excommunication and the hope for their conversion. Against the Salvadoran president he leveled the charge of being a liar, for in his recent visit to Mexico he had denied any persecution of the church by his government. Something he said will be a source of courage for me for as long as I live. He pointed to the escalating brutality of the persecutors, who thought that by greater violence they could terrorize the persecuted to the point of leaving them incapable of thinking, saying or doing anything contrary to their terrorizers. He went on, "If we should oblige them, they will have won. But I do not believe the murder of these five has been in vain. They have preceded us in the experience of the resurrection. We live by that power that even death cannot destroy. We honor them and our faith by living unafraid, by knowing that evil has no future."

We embraced again, a Catholic prelate and a Presbyterian layman. I thought then and many times afterward that Christian unity is never stronger than when it is sealed by the blood of the martyrs. Somehow that moment made me forever a member of Monseñor's flock and, as never before, a member of the universal body of Christ.

Monseñor left for Puebla shortly after Mass, but not before entrusting me to the care of some of his closest friends. He went to Mexico bearing the cost of his flock's fidelity, supremely signified in the growing number of his martyrs.

The body of one of them was not obtained by his family until late Sunday night. His family had heard me over the radio. They sent for me asking that I lead a funeral for him. I was warned that informers would be present. Armed with Monseñor's call to courage in the face of terrorizers, I did go, together with some dozen Baptist young adults. It was a simple Protestant service of hymns, Bible reading, and a sermon. Roberto was only sixteen. I was nearly overcome with anger when his mother asked me to see him in the open coffin. But in the manner of Monseñor, I preached hope and forgiveness, but also determination that the blood of these martyrs would become the seed of a new and just society; otherwise we might trivialize both their life and death.

Born in Mexico, many years later naturalized as a United States citizen, I felt that night Salvadoran through and through, but in the manner of those who daily struggle to see God's Kingdom displace the legacy of dictators and the barbarity of puppet regimes—in other words, a Salvadoran molded by Monseñor's example.

We corresponded sporadically in the months that followed. I sent him personal messages with friends traveling to El Salvador, and he always returned them with special words of affection. Some time in the early fall of that year, 1979, a number of us in New York formalized to him an invitation to be our keynote speaker at the semiannual meeting of the Governing Board of the National Council of Churches to be held in early November. He accepted gladly, with one reservation: if his people were in any danger he might have to cancel the trip.

The dictatorship of Carlos Humberto Romero was toppled in a bloodless coup on October 15. It was chiefly the work of younger military officers, many of them sympathetic to Monseñor's positions. He went on radio the next day to ask the nation to give the new civilian-military junta its cooperation for a probational period. The civilians in the new government, with the exception of one or two, were distinguished Salvadorans of unimpeachable credentials. He was criticized for what appeared naiveté. The critics turned out to be right. Within days, the old guard of the military forces overruled the younger officers and the illustrious civilians. Peaceful demonstrations were quelled with unprecedented ferocity. One massacre followed another. Monseñor Romero denounced the violence in no uncertain terms, but as a peacemaker, hopeful that the more humane elements of the government would check or eliminate the barbarians, he kept on speaking of the "church's conditional cooperation." But he was also a realist. A few weeks later he withdrew from the junta any support whatsoever. That was the signal for the distinguished civilians to resign.

On the eve of his departure for New York, he called me to tell me he could not possibly come. The next day would be critical. A coalition of opposition groups (whose rights to organize he defended to the end) were to stage a protest march through the city. A similar march ten days before had been fired upon by the National Guard. Nearly one hundred had been killed and scores wounded. To avert a repetition, he was planning to march with the protesters. He also had to negotiate the release of three government officials held hostage for three weeks.

I assured him the National Council of Churches would not only understand, but thank him for his pastoral example. So would thousands of Hispanics who were planning to attend an ecumenical mass we had organized for him at St. Patrick's Cathedral. I did ask him to let us tape a message from him for the two gatherings. That we did through special equipment.

The Mass was held with an overflow crowd. The Governing Board of the National Council did in fact draft a message of support and congratulations for his pastoral integrity. I was delegated to carry that message to him in person and arranged by telephone with him to spend a week with him to highlight the companionship of U.S. Hispanics and the National Council with the Salvadoran church.

That week was in mid-November. He received me with a combination of paternal and fraternal affection. Except for times when he dealt with confidential matters, I spent every day with him from early morning until past midnight.

First came my reading of the message at the 8 o'clock Mass on Sunday, broadcast to the rest of the nation through YSAX. Part of the message, enthusiastically applauded, was a pledge by the National Council to be especially vigilant in seeing to it that our government would no longer support totalitarian regimes, but only those that upheld authentic human rights.

On the ensuing days he took me to visit *comunidades eclesiales de base* (grassroots church communities) to enjoy with him patron saints' festivities, to share pastoral planning sessions with priests, lay people, and members of religious orders, to speak to the seminarians, and beginning at 6:30 every morning, to attend Mass where he began his day as a pastor, in the chapel of the Divine Providence. His congregation were the terminal cancer patients of the adjourning hospital run by the sisters of Divine Providence, and the sisters themselves. Our best time was following that Mass, when we went across the street for a leisurely breakfast served in the hospital refectory by the sisters, who also joined actively in the conversation. Here he was relaxed, humorous, talkative, and even mildly critical of his critics.

I was of course impressed by many aspects of his personality after a week of such close companionship. His intellect was keen, his memory enormous, his capacity for work prodigious, his political instincts astute, his love for his flock boundless. And yet, there remained etched on his face a hint of infinite sadness. In retrospect I think I know what that was.

Of course, he was mortified by the continuing violence of the government's armed forces and the government's unwillingness or incapacity to control the equally brutal violence coming from the extreme right and its paramilitary groups. Also, he agonized over the division in the episcopate. Only Bishop Arturo Rivera y Damas shared his views. The other four (together we nicknamed them the "angelicals") were openly antagonistic.

But there was more. I learned from many of his friends that the threats on his life were frequent and ominous. As we were leaving a group of leaders of *comunidades de base*, an elderly woman pled with him to take care of himself. I had observed others making the same plea repeatedly. In a moment of privacy, I asked him if he thought of protecting himself. He said he would not. How could he do it when his own people had no such security? How could he, when his very spiritual life derived from that open, daily replenishment with his brothers and sisters? Besides, the very vulnerability of his flock was a direct result of their believing and acting what he preached. He told me he had never loved life more.

It was a springtime of faith and courage for the church in El Salvador. It had never been more alive. It was as if with each new torture, exile, or assassination, the community's resolve to be more faithful multiplied. No, he had no appetite to be a martyr, but if he were to become one, he prayed that the circumstances would leave no doubt as to his vocation: to be a servant of God and a pastor to his flock.

Months later, on March 24 in the early evening, I was in Washington, D.C., finishing the testimony I was to present to a subcommittee of the House of Representatives against military aid to El Salvador. The phone rang. At the other end was a Baptist calling me from San Salvador. "Jorge, Jorge, *our* Monseñor was assassinated an hour ago," he blurted. I collapsed with wracking sobs, managing finally to ask him, "Where did it happen?" He told me. He was saying a memorial Mass at the little chapel of the Divine Providence for the mother of a journalist friend.

Days later I further found out that the assassin's bullet went through his heart just as he was finishing the words of the institution of the Eucharist: "This is my body which will be given up for you. . . . This is the cup of my blood . . . shed for you. . . ." I felt a strange sense of joy. God had granted his wish.

Since then I have often addressed audiences about him and his church. Remembering how he lived and died, I have dared to say: Together with thousands of Salvadorans I have seen Jesus. This time his name was Oscar Arnulfo Romero. His broken body is broken with the body of Jesus; his shed blood is shed with the blood of Jesus. And as with Jesus, so it is with Monseñor, he died for us so that we might live in freedom and in love and justice for one another. His resurrection is not a future event. It is a present reality. He is life for us now, and that is why we must defeat the forces of death in El Salvador and wherever Jesus continues to be crucified.

I was at his funeral, leading a delegation of three from the National Council of Churches. Again the barbarians unleashed their violence against Monseñor's friends. In death he was a greater threat to them than in life. So they broke up his funeral Mass with bombs and machinegun fire. They caused another massacre. But their victory was momentary. Now, driven to insurrection, Salvadorans will yet bring to fruition Monseñor's oblation, "Let my blood be the seed of freedom." We, Monseñor's friends in the United States, are caught up in the hope of his oblation, and judging from the signs of the time, we have much work to do.

JORGE LARA-BRAUD
Director,
Council on Theology and Culture,
Presbyterian Church in the U.S.

Translators' Preface

Readers not familiar with the history of El Salvador may be helped by a brief description of the historico-political background and of the major forces at work on the contemporary scene.

In 1932 a popular insurrection took place in El Salvador. Its main leader was Farabundo Martí, an internationalist and socialist. The insurrection was put down with violence. Some thirty thousand persons were killed. Since that time the nation has been governed by the armed forces and real power held by a ruling oligarchy constituted by fourteen Salvadoran families.

In reaction to the violent repression and economic monopolization that have continued to characterize Salvadoran life, various opposition groups have been organized along geographical or occupational lines *(campesinos,* factory workers, students). Some of these groups, in time, faded away, while others have flourished.

All major oppositional organizations today, including official political opposition parties, are united in a broad coalition against the existing power structure. This political coalition is called the FDR, *Frente Democrático Revolucionario* (Democratic Revolutionary Front). It would form the government in El Salvador upon the dissolution of the present government. There is also a military coalition called the FMLN, *Frente Farabundo Martí para la Liberación Nacional* (Farabundo Martí National Liberation Front). With a change in government, this front would become the people's army.

As in all other Latin American nations, a central role in El Salvador's history has been played by the Roman Catholic Church, both the institutional church, with its official, visible structures, and "the people's church," largely organized in the "Christian base communities."

Some of the terminology used in the Latin American church calls for a brief explanation for English-language readers.

The **"movement—or march forward, or mobilization, or initiative—of the poor"** *(proyecto histórico de los empobrecidos):* the historical development of a society as it struggles to attain a socio-political configuration in keeping with the dictates of the kingdom of God. It includes the effort to overcome injustice and oppression and the will to create a society where the majority will not be dominated by a minority, a society of equal rights for all, in fellowship.

"Base, or basic, communities" *(comunidades de base):* small groups of Christians who come together for study, group discussion, training, social action projects, or worship. They represent a yearning for authentic Christian (ecclesial) life apart from, but not necessarily in opposition to, official (ecclesiastical) structures.

In El Salvador, as elsewhere, these communities are small: fifty families would be a maximum. The base communities generally make use of four service positions or ministries. A *priest* directs the parish work of the group. A *coordinator* directs the community activities. A *catechist* teaches Christian doctrine and is in charge of Christian education, not only of children but of the entire community, young and old. *Lay ministers* (both men and women) conduct the weekly celebration of the word of God, at which a priest may or may not be present. The lay minister *(celebrador de la Palabra)* does everything a priest might do, except the sacramental functions proper to the priesthood.

"New (regenerated, renewed) person, new society." This is a term popularized by Ernesto "Che" Guevara to typify the person who is both progenitor and child of a more just and equitable social order. It refers to a person or society with a commitment to social justice, oriented to the common good of the social collectivity, motivated by love and commitment to other persons, in solidarity with them.

"The poor." Plácido Erdozaín rarely uses the common Spanish word for poor, *pobre.* He prefers the term *empobrecido;* it implies something more than simply the state or condition of poverty: it implies that that condition has been *imposed* on the person in it. The poor are not simply poor: they are *made to be* poor, poverty is imposed on them. The closest English equivalent would probably be the past-participial form "impoverished," but we have generally used the word "poor" in our translation, though it lacks the full depth of *empobrecido*.

Campesino. The dictionary equivalent in English is "peasant," but this is a word that hardly figures in the active vocabulary of contemporary English-language speakers, and it conjures up a medieval, European image. The word *campesino* is cognate with *campo,* "field," "land." A *campesino* is someone who lives from the land, the fields; a landworker. In Latin America, poor *campesinos* own very little land and so are unable to support themselves and their families from their own holdings. They are thus totally dependent on nearby landowners, in one or another arrangement that almost invariably drives them deeper and deeper into deprivation, indebtedness, desperation, and readiness for change. In our translation we have used the terms "landworker" and "peasant" very seldom—only in contexts where the word *campesino* runs the risk of not making the author's point. For the rest, we opt for the Spanish term, suggesting a way of life virtually absent from and unfamiliar to the English-speaking world.

In many cases in the text, priests who continue to work in El Salvador or other places in Central America are mentioned. The author has chosen not to use their real names, or uses their *noms de guerre*, to protect their continuing work in the region. This is also the case of some lay people mentioned. They are all very real people and in no way would we want this document to be used against them.

"*There can be no church unity if we ignore the world in which we live.*"

Acronyms

BPR, *Bloque Popular Revolucionario,* Popular Revolutionary Bloc

CCS, *Consejo Coordinador de Sindicatos,* Labor Union Coordinating Council

CELAM, *Conferencia Episcopal Latinoamericana,* Latin American Episcopal Conference

CONIP, *Coordinadora Nacional de la Iglesia Popular,* National Coordinating Committee of the People's Church

COSDO, *Consejo Sindical de Oriente,* Eastern Labor Union Council

CRM, *Coordinadora Revolucionaria de Masas,* Mass Revolutionary Coordinating Committee

CUTS, *Confederación Unitaria de Trabajadores Salvadoreños,* Unified Salvadoran Workers' Confederation

FAPU, *Frente de Acción Popular Unificada,* Popular Unified Action Front

FDR, *Frente Democrático Revolucionario,* Democratic Revolutionary Front

FMLN, *Frente Farabundo Martí para la Liberación Nacional,* Farabundo Martí National Liberation Front

FPL, *Fuerzas Populares de Liberación,* The People's Liberation Forces

GRP, *Grupo de Reflexión Pastoral,* Pastoral Reflection Group

PDC, *Partido Demócrata Cristiano,* Christian Democratic Party

UCA, *Universidad Centroamericana,* University of Central America

UDN, *Unión Democrática Nacionalista,* Nationalist Democratic Union

UNO, *Unión Nacional de la Oposición,* National Opposition Union

UTC, *Unión de Trabajadores del Campo,* Landworkers' Union

"As a shepherd, I am obliged by divine law to give my life for those I love, for the entire Salvadoran people, including those Salvadorans who threaten to assassinate me."

I

Elements of a Portrait

We want to sketch for you a portrait of our martyred bishop, Oscar Arnulfo Romero. Of necessity, it will be a one-sided portrait, because it is put together from one specific point of view, but there was no other way *we* could do it.

Our point of view is that of a team of priests called the Pastoral Reflection Group (GRP, *Grupo de Reflexión Pastoral)*. Since 1970 we have been working with Salvadoran "base communities"—small, informal, Christian-oriented groups for discussion, action, and worship—within the historical movement forward of the poor in our country.

Our relations with Bishop Romero were a bit prickly in the beginning. In 1972, as a result of the military invasion of the university premises and our support of the people, we had a difficult meeting with him. At that time he was auxiliary bishop to Bishop Luis Chávez. When later he was named archbishop he told us, "My job was to finish you off." But the shared practical experiences of the next three years brought us closer and closer together. We came to the point where we really appreciated and loved him.

On February 6, 1980, on his return from Europe, we met him at the airport. He told us with a smile on his face: "I'm beginning to understand something: communion with a bishop should not be vertical or static; it should be dynamic and reciprocal—dialectical." We were the only ones who really knew how much it meant for him to say that.

There is no doubt that we were in a kind of give-and-take communion with him and that we learned a great deal from him. The

1

major thing for us was that he made it easier to express and exercise fidelity to the gospel and to the poor of our country as we lived in the midst of persecution and dealt with the crisis caused by the deaths of six priests and hundreds of Christian and non-Christian friends.

It is from this perspective that we see Bishop Romero's assassination as a martyrdom, as one more episode in a struggle between the gods: the god of Cain, of the pharaohs, of Caesar, of an oppressive economic system fighting it out with the God of the poor, the God whom Jesus calls Father.

Our bishop offered his life to the God of the poor, and the god of the empire gave the order "Kill him!" for being "blasphemous," for coming from "Galilee" and "raising the people's consciousness" of their real situation. If the empire's servants allowed him to live, they could no longer call themselves "friends of Caesar."

Bishop Oscar Romero had already offered his life and, for that reason, they could not take it away from him. They could only steal it from his people. That is why his death remains part of the life of the people massacred on the streets and sidewalks of El Salvador.

We know that the portrait we draw is incomplete. No one has the whole truth. Christians believe that truth, unity, justice, and love are parts of a historical projection that we are always reaching for. From the future it beckons us to do what we must in order to create it. Little by little it will become clear as part of the total process that is the liberation of our people.

The Context

El Salvador is the smallest republic in the Americas: 8,260 square miles—the size of Massachusetts. It is the only country in Central America with no Caribbean coast and no banana export trade. Chilean poet Gabriela Mistral called it "the Tom Thumb of America." Five million individuals trying to be a people.

But since 1932 a military dictatorship has not let them be a people. Thirty thousand lives were lost in putting an end to the insurrection, the first attempt at socialism in the hemisphere.

And since then the dead have added up to thousands more. El Salvador is now steeped in blood and suffering the agony of a difficult labor as it gives birth to a regenerated people.

Adapting the words of our great poet Roque Dalton, we can say of El Salvador:

> Official language: Spanish, although officials speak English quite well.
>
> Government: counterrevolutionary junta made up of military men and Christian Democrats. They give the orders in El Salvador, but they get their instructions from Washington.
>
> History: too much like that of the rest of Latin America. Enough said.
>
> Currency: the *colón,* even though the money that rules the roost is the good old American dollar.
>
> The laws are made by the rich to be followed by the poor. When the poor make the laws, the rich class will disappear.

Here are the names of the famous fourteen families, the rulers (as long as the Yankees keep them there) of the destiny of El Salvador: Llach, De Sola, Hill, Dueñas, Regalado, Wright, Salaverría, García Prieto, Quiñónes, Guirola, Borja, Sol, Daglio, and Meza Ayau.

Facts and Figures

- Half of the population lives on less than $10 a month.
- Only 16 percent of the work force have year-round employment.
- Half of 1 percent of all landowners own 38 percent of the arable land, whereas the poorer 91 percent own only 23 percent of the land.
- Salvadorans have put up with fifty years of military tyranny that gets worse as the economic crisis grows and the reforms designed to fool the people fail, one by one.
- Three-fifths of the rural population and two-fifths of the urban do not know how to read or write.

Our Hope

As of 1980, the Salvadoran people are solidly organized around the Democratic Revolutionary Front (FDR, *Frente Democrático Revolucionario)* and its vanguard the Farabundo Martí National Liberation Front (FMLN, *Frente Farabundo Martí para la Liberación Nacional).*

Our hope is for solidarity among all peoples of the world—with great faith in God, in the people, and in the future of a liberated Latin America.

Milestones in the Bishop's Life

Chronology may not explain anything of a person's life. As one of Victor Jara's songs says, "Life is eternal in five minutes." Christian thinkers distinguish between chronological time and "kairotic" time—time beyond measure . . . the moment of encounter . . . the "opportune time." However, a chronology may give us some clues for interpretation.

Oscar Arnulfo Romero y Galdámez came into this world in 1917 in Ciudad Barrios, in the department of San Miguel on the border with Honduras. His father: Santos Romero, a telegraph operator. His mother: Guadalupe de Jesús, a saint.

When he was quite young he began his studies with the Claretian Fathers. Later he entered the seminary in San Salvador.

In 1942 he was ordained to the priesthood.

In 1943 he entered the Gregorian University in Rome. He obtained the licentiate degree in theology. He did not have time to do his doctoral thesis. It was one of those things he was always "going" to do. (It might not be a bad idea for the doyens of Rome's Gregorian University to take a look at his "complete works"— the sermons and pastoral letters—and award him a doctorate in theology posthumously.)

Parish priest of Anamorós, secretary to Bishop Machado, rector of the cathedral, director of the San Miguel Seminary, and rector of the Interdiocesan Seminary in San Salvador.

1966, secretary general of the Episcopal Conference of El Salvador.

1967, executive secretary of the Episcopal Council of Central America and Panama.

May 3, 1970, auxiliary bishop to Luís Chávez in San Salvador.

October 15, 1974, bishop of Santiago de María (aristocratic coffee growers on one side, indigent rural proletariat on the other).

February 3, 1977, appointed archbishop of San Salvador. He took possession from Archbishop Chávez on February 22.

March 24, 1980, death and resurrection! Archbishop Romero was shot to death at the altar of the chapel in the Divine Providence Cancer Hospital run by the Carmelite nuns.

He lives on in the liberation struggle of our people. That is why the people took to the streets *en masse* that day, shouting: "Comrade Oscar Romero! Onward to victory forever!"

February 8, 1977—Meeting in Santa Lucía

The country was in the midst of an electoral campaign. The popular movement had decided not to participate in the elections because of repeated frauds; elections were nothing but an organized lie.

On February 8, 1977, the Pastoral Reflection Group held a meeting in the church of Santa Lucía. It was an emergency meeting provoked by a series of events that we felt we had to deal with in a way that would be both Christian and militant.

On January 11 a bomb had been placed in Father Alfonso Navarro's house in Miramonte (he was later assassinated, May 11).

Father Garo's house was machinegunned and the walls of his church in Opico were painted with accusations and threats. He was one of us. The assault was carried out by soldiers dressed as civilians: they were acting out the lie that there was no connection between the military and extreme rightist groups.

In January Mario Bernal, the priest in Apopa, had been tortured. He was then expelled from the country.

And we still had the nagging problem of Aguilares, where the organized Christian communities, and especially Father Rutilio Grande (who would be assassinated on March 12), were being accused of the death of a landowner.

We had analyzed the situation as "organized and systematic persecution," but our bishops, and many others, considered all of these events isolated incidents.

We all entered the meeting wielding that day's newspaper, with questions on our faces.

On the front page was the classic photograph of our retiring bishop, Luis Chávez, dressed in a cassock, smiling. Next to him, with his typical half-smile, was what we were worried about: Oscar Arnulfo Romero y Galdámez, the new archbishop of San Salvador.

There were eight of us at the meeting, all priests. More than half of us had seriously considered the alternative of going somewhere else, where we would be able to do pastoral work among and with the people—the people's church. But our decision on that could wait. We were in a hurry to share what we knew about the new archbishop and figure out what the immediate future held for us.

I had known Bishop Romero for a long time. He had been a member of the cursillo movement *(Cursillos de Cristiandad)* from the very beginning and recently had felt attracted to the spirituality of the conservative Opus Dei. Churchy, lover of rules and clerical discipline, friend of liturgical laws, he was convinced that "the most important thing is prayer and personal conversion."

He thought that the glory of God was reflected in the glory and purity of the church, and he really suffered when he had to cover up the sins of the institution—his task when he served as secretary to the bishop of his diocese, with all its weaknesses. But behind the rationalizations he was himself honest to the core and free. He suffered from nervous tension caused by the strain of cloaking the defects of the institutional church, while maintaining his own integrity.

José, a priest who works with the *campesinos*—landless rural working people—told us how Bishop Romero was an auxiliary bishop to Luis Chávez in San Salvador. Because of his condition, or his conditioning, he could not keep up with the pace set by the archbishop and the other auxiliary bishop, Arturo Rivera y Damas, and he was relegated to less strategic tasks: works of charity, the nuns, the communication media, and the like. On the occasion of the military intervention at the National University he confronted our Christian communities with the accusation of getting mixed up in politics and of losing our Christian identity. The conflict was so serious that we even questioned whether we should celebrate the Eucharist with him.

Roberto, a priest from the diocese of Santiago de María, told us that Romero was an introvert. When he had a problem, he would shut himself up alone in his room, pray, study, and then try to solve it by episcopal *fiat*. Roberto insisted, however, that Romero was very honest, had a tremendous capacity for work, and thought for himself. He spoke to us of his huge but carefully selected library of works in theology in general and pastoral theology in particular. When he was at the Gregorian University in Rome he was known for being very studious, an orderly, logical thinker.

He became secretary general of the Episcopal Conference of El Salvador and was transferred from San Miguel at the time of the arrival of the Franciscan bishop, Graciano. Later, he became the executive secretary of the Episcopal Council of Central America and Panama.

Next he was named bishop of Santiago de María, an area of coffee-growing highlands and cotton-growing coastal plain. He came to take over for an eccentric whom we called the "lion of Judah," Bishop Francisco Castro, who claimed that because he had not signed the documents of the Latin American Episcopal Conference at Medellín, he therefore was not obliged to carry them out. We knew that in Santiago some high-ranking military officers used him as a consultant.

At that time Romero believed that the church was made up of the "good rich" and the "good poor," and he put as much distance as possible between himself and the "bad rich" and the revolutionary poor—as so many parishes and hierarchs still do.

It looked as if our kind of pastoral work, which involved working directly with the poor, was going to be fenced in.

But Father Neto Barrera (killed on November 28, 1978), a real radical but also a solid realist, convinced us that Bishop Romero was the best of a bad lot inasmuch as he had a great advantage over the others: he was honest and he wanted to be faithful to his Christian commitment. We all would have preferred that Rivera be chosen, but he had a history of problems with Rome and so he was out of the running.

We determined to use what was available, rather than to avoid the issue. Our job was to offer Bishop Romero our experience with the people and show him how one can live one's faith in the midst of the people's struggle, along with our Christian communities.

Xavier, another *campesino* priest, in a flash of "prophetic illumination" said:

> Look, we keep on with our work in the Christian communities and keep identifying ourselves with the needs and struggles of the people. You know that Bishop Romero, even in the short period that he worked as auxiliary bishop, showed signs of having very delicate health; so let's leave it at that. It's only a matter of time; his health is poor and he won't be able to handle the enormous amount of work in the archdiocese. Besides, we are men of faith, and I'm sure that the Holy Spirit won't let us down.

Two years later a great friendship had developed between Xavier and Bishop Romero, in part because of the persecution they were both enduring. Xavier tells the story that one time, at the end of an intense day of pastoral work, which involved visiting rural Christian communities, he was impressed by the serenity, energy, and good humor of Bishop Romero. "How is it possible that before you became archbishop your health was very delicate and now, with three times the work, you don't even catch a cold?" Our bishop, with that profound faith of his, answered: "How about that? I guess God knows what he's doing!"

During that two-hour meeting we went over the whole history of Bishop Romero. In the end the balance was swaying back and forth between dread and hope.

We then had only a little time left to put the finishing touches on a "statement of faith" that had been prepared by the priests of Nejapa in response to the government's moves against our communities. We also had to prepare a communiqué condemning two organizations that represented the interests of the ruling class. The communiqué would then be studied and discussed in the base communities.

February 13, 1977—Demonstration in Apopa

This time the meeting place for the communities was Apopa. We gathered at the gas station just outside the town. Our purpose was to protest the expulsion of Father Mario Bernal and the campaign unleashed against us by the landowners. The fourteen priests who were to celebrate Mass put on their albs and stoles and joined the ranks of the communities. We followed behind the pole with the two loudspeakers on it and the four persons who were carrying the batteries on a stretcher. Marchers were singing and shouting slogans: "The church cannot be silenced by tanks and machineguns!"; "Blessed are the poor for they shall build the Kingdom of God!" In four strategic places in the town we came to a stop for a reading of the Word and comments by one of the lay ministers. The stop in front of the army garrison was very tense but the woman who commented on the reading did not back down or wince; the guards retreated into the garrison.

Someone came from taking a head count: "There's more than six thousand!"

And after the procession, the Eucharist. There were too many of us to fit into the church and so we celebrated Mass in the plaza, lighted by the sun and humming with the sounds of marketplace bustle. And in the midst of all that came the homily by Rutilio Grande, the sermon on Cain and Abel, in which he stated: "It is practically illegal to be a Christian in this country." (Could this homily have been his death sentence?)

After Mass, inside the church that we used as our sacristy, Rutilio encouraged us to trust Bishop Romero. The truth is that the problem of the new bishop was on all of our minds.

As I left I came across Carmelo, whom I had not seen since 1974. He signaled me to stay quiet. "Please, Father, don't use my name! Be careful; we've detected a number of government informants, and they've been taking pictures." He was one of the Christians from the early days of the community when we approached popular organizations with hesitancy and fear. He had opted for armed struggle, and it was he who first gave me a copy of the diary of the Bolivian Christian guerrilla Néstor Paz.

The installation of Bishop Romero was planned to be a solemn occasion, according to all the rules and formalities. But the government thought that the interregnum would be an opportune moment for its interests, and it thought it could "count on" the new bishop. The government began an escalation of repression against the church. It was aimed especially at certain priests who worked in the city of San Salvador, whom government officials considered to be the worst troublemakers. They took advantage of the situation to capture, torture, and expel Guillermo Denoux (a Belgian), as well as Bernard and John (Americans). The latter were expelled from the country with the complicity of the papal nuncio.

For Rafael Barahona, a Salvadoran priest who worked with the *campesinos,* the repression was much more cruel. When they brought him back to the chancery, he had been severely beaten. The guards had taken out all their fury on his body.

Archbishop Luis Chávez was grief-stricken with helplessness and begged Bishop Romero to take his place quickly. The ceremony was short and almost private, in the church of San José de la Montaña, just in time for the beginning of a new massacre of the people.

February 28, 1977—Massacre in Plaza Libertad

Bishop Romero had said that the rhythm of the church in San Salvador had to be kept up, and he wanted to carry on the program of clergy formation that had been planned the year before. On March 1 a three-day workshop was to begin, to study the infiltration of imperialist ideology through certain religious sects and reformist movements that had the effect of sidetracking the people from involvement in their own real-life struggle.

Very few priests showed up that morning. Some came because they did not know what had happened the day before; others of us came because we *did* know what had happened and we wanted to see what we could do together about it—the massacre in Plaza Libertad on February 28.

After opening statements (Rutilio Grande spoke on the first theme, as scheduled), we asked that the day's agenda be changed.

This was Bishop Romero's first meeting with his clergy. In a way we were testing him. And he passed the test.

We shared with the others what we had found out. The three official opposition political parties had occupied Plaza Libertad (San Salvador) for six days, in protest against the blatant fraud in the recent elections. The Christian Democratic Party (PDC), Nationalist Democratic Union (UDN), and National Revolutionary Movement (MNR) made up the National Opposition Union (UNO) and were the opposition parties that took part in the elections; other movements and organizations refused to participate.

Approximately ten thousand persons had gathered there on that day. The plaza was completely encircled by the National Guard. The massacre took place that night, as the guardsmen started shooting. Thousands took refuge in the church of Rosario, there on Plaza Libertad.

A priest who had been involved in the whole thing was Octavio Ortiz, from the parish of Mejicanos (assassinated January 20, 1979). Part of his community was there too. They got out the best way they could, although escape seemed almost impossible. Most of those who tried to escape were captured by the time they reached Plaza Zurita; they were taken to prison. Octavio left his car, and another registered in Guillermo's name, nearby.

Octavio was a man of few words in public; later he told us, on the side, that at midnight the guards started shooting indiscriminately. Soon the trucks started to arrive to pick up the dead and wounded, and the water trucks to clean up the blood. The Red Cross was nowhere to be seen. Those who could took refuge in the church of Rosario; those who did not make it were killed. They threw gas into the church and it was a real hell in there, but the self-control and discipline of the people was admirable. Octavio took the risk of trying to escape, and he made it.

Bishop Chávez was asked to mediate; he told us about that. They called on him to take Bishop Romero's place, because Romero had gone to Santiago de María to transport his personal belongings. The church was encircled. Chávez went in with the Red Cross to get party leaders out safely.

Bishop Romero listened to this in silence. It was clear that he wanted to do the right thing. Then the story was told of the Mass the day before in the middle of the plaza. Those who were occupying the plaza had asked that a Mass be said there, because it was Sunday.

It was decided that it would be possible, but that it would have to be led by a Salvadoran priest. Alfonso Navarro got his things and prepared to preside over the celebration. There was nothing really strange about this decision. The majority of those gathered there were Christians. They were celebrating the liturgy of a people painfully forging their own history. In this struggle the values of the kingdom to come are usually implicit only, and it was now time to make them explicit and concrete. Alfonso made this clarification beautifully, with the entire plaza ringed by the National Guard. It was a very tense situation. Alfonso told us that his whole body was trembling. At the end of the Mass he said, "And if they kill me now, you know who is responsible." (And they did kill him, on May 12 that year.)

During the Mass, Christian youth groups of the base communities distributed more than ten thousand copies of Guillermo Denoux's letter to the people gathered in the plaza. The letter said, "Finally the church is where it always should have been: with the people, surrounded by wolves."

Then we all looked at the new archbishop. He only listened and asked questions. Finally he surprised all of us:

> Let's stop talking. The meeting is over. Everyone go home to take care of the people. Open your houses to any who think they are in danger. Check to see if they are really being followed, and, if they are, take them in and hide them. I will be in the meeting room at the chancery all morning. Everyone who has news or needs to find out what is going on should come. We will be there trying to figure out the situation and making plans based on what we find out.

We looked at each other, surprised and smiling. We went back to our posts filled with hope. When we got to our house, two of the leaders were already there asking to be taken in.

Almost none of our communities had participated in the elections because, since 1974, we had decided in favor of extraparliamentary struggle. But now we had a new date for the people never

to forget: February 28. And a new hope: Bishop Oscar Arnulfo
Romero.

March 12, 1977—Rutilio Grande, Martyr

On the sidewalks of El Salvador you hear peasant voices or
loud transistors tuned to YSAX, the Catholic radio station, singing:

> On the 12th of March,
> that unforgettable date,
> they killed our brother,
> Father Rutilio Grande.

On that day I was coming back from celebrating a wedding in
the community and found Ricardo, alone and crying. He said,
"They've killed Rutilio." I tried to find a word of comfort.
Nothing. "Let's go," he said. By the time we got to Delgado he
had an idea. "I think we should go and get on the radio." We
headed for YSAX. We told the employees that we came by orders
of the archbishop.

We did not know a thing about radio programing, but we
created an intense three-hour special. They told me to coordinate things: Ricardo—meditations; Yolanda—biblical readings;
Jorge—songs. And that is how the new YSAX was born, the voice
of the Panamerican people. And the church entered a new phase.

We arrived at Aguilares—where Rutilio had been pastor—
about midnight. The people had left because the communities and
the leadership felt that for reasons of security they should not
hold large gatherings at night.

Bishop Romero was there. A profound silence enveloped him.
He had said Mass and now was asking something about an
autopsy. As he passed by he looked into the poor and empty room
used by Rutilio, the first Salvadoran Jesuit to work directly with
the rural poor, the *campesinos*. He had given everything he had to
his work with the people, the poor. He courageously searched out
new paths to follow. All of us accepted him as a good man, an
example of the reawakened, dedicated Christian.

We walked closer and I heard our bishop say simply, "He was poor." That must have been very important to him. When he saw us coming he put his arm around the shoulders of each one of us as if we were Rutilio's relatives. The corpses of Rutilio, Nelson, and Manuel—his two *campesino* friends murdered with him— were on the floor of the church, covered only by blood-stained sheets. The people were singing songs of revolutionary struggle and hope.

A number of changes occurred in Bishop Romero and the direction of the Salvadoran church as a result of Rutilio's death.

First, a break with the ruling-class idea of legality. In Apopa, Rutilio had already said that "being Christian means being illegal. . . ." Another good man from Aguilares had written a theological analysis of legality and evangelization in El Salvador. Its publication was blocked at the last minute. But Bishop Romero was able to express its ideas by simple actions, which included burying Rutilio and his martyred companions in the chapel of El Paisnal without waiting for governmental permission. And he called for public demonstrations despite the state of seige—which included prohibition of public gatherings—imposed since the massacre on February 28.

Second, a break with certain assumptions about Christianity. Dialogue between the government and the church as two "self-sufficient" societies was broken; the church stationed itself "with the people, surrounded by wolves"—well aware of the possible consequences.

Our bishop sent a letter to President Molina telling him that the church would not appear in any official government activity as long as the facts about Rutilio's assassination were not clarified. Soon he added other conditions to be met before the church would engage in any further dialogue with the government: permission for the return of all priests who had been expelled or had re-entry permissions denied, and the end of all repression of the people. He wanted action, not promises. There would be no return to the old type of dialogue. His demands would have to be met before *any kind* of dialogue would be considered.

Third, the new liturgy. A new liturgy was already in use, and that is a long story in itself. New Christian attitudes demanded new ways of celebrating the Word. The Eucharist was celebrated at the end of demonstrations, and sometimes even during them, during land takeovers, and when the people took over vacant lots to build places to live. It began to be necessary to receive the sacraments only under the strictest security measures and in "safe" houses. And there were new celebrations, such as "the liturgy of maize." But in the entire history of El Salvador, liturgy was never discussed as it was when Bishop Romero decreed that there would be only one Mass celebrated in the entire archdiocese on that Sunday, the ninth-day remembrance of Rutilio's death.

The decision was made to close all Catholic schools for three days and send home with each student a discussion guide about the situation of the church and how it was being persecuted. A lists of points was drawn up on martyrdom, Christian communities, and the Eucharist. They were broadcast on the radio and distributed to all the small, base communities for discussion. The culmination would be the prohibition of other Masses on that Sunday. (The bourgeoisie screamed: "mortal sin, sacrilege, especially now that we need to pray more than ever before!")

And there was no other celebration of the Eucharist in the archdiocese that day; parishioners had to come to the archdiocesan Mass. It was a marvel to see the huge multitude of faithful in the plaza in front of the cathedral. The people understood the gesture and felt strengthened. (I still remember the spontaneous reaction of the people when they refused to let the Red Cross take care of those who fainted, because the Red Cross had not cared for the wounded after the massacre on February 28. The people did this themselves.)

Some persons who did not understand the language of symbolism complained that Bishop Romero did not take the opportunity to make an all-out denunciation of the situation. They did not know about the pressure that was on him. Both the upper classes and the government had put the heat on to cancel the Mass because they saw it as a political gesture that could lead to popular insurrection. Some sectors of the church gave arguments based on canon law about having to go to Mass on Sunday. And for our bishop: a baptism by fire, his first fight on the side of the people, on the side of the poor.

Fourth, a new basis for church unity. For a long time our church had been going through a vigorous process of aggiornamento, as it was called then. It was a modern, organic church. For example, after a year of preparation we had two weeks of what we called "pastoral studies" as a way to maneuver around the canonical obstacles associated with formal meetings, and we were able to create a *true* diocesan synod.

Our church was also very militant and involved. Romero had been named to put the brakes on that, and he had been disposed to do so. But as a result of Rutilio's death, mass meetings of priests, nuns, and laypersons began and we started to act together. We still have many conflicts and internal divisions, but we have no time now to keep on discussing doctrine. Everyone has to take a side. You are either with the poor or against them. That is how a new kind of unity began to grow—a unity that will continue to expand even as it brings out the objective divisions that are not resolved at any given time.

Fifth, a new service to the people. Our church has always thought of the poor in terms of helping them, supporting cooperatives, preaching "social doctrine," and so forth. But now the church has opened to a dialogue of equals with the organizations that totally belong to the poor, their revolutionary movement. Some say that "the church has given the streets back to the people," because the huge celebrations of the Eucharist give these organizations a chance to move around and spread information. Others believe that the church is now "the voice of those who have no voice," and lends its meetings and means of communication to them so that the people's organizations can speak when there is no other way to do so. The public statements of the bishop began to reflect the perspective of the poor. But there was nothing simple about this development. The bishop did not really understand it himself. Many intelligent priests, in favor of modernization, thought of the demonstrations during religious ceremonies and the sharing of political information during them as somehow disrespectful. They could not understand that we were living under circumstances of institutionalized violence that robbed the people of their right to speak, the result of a long and convulsive history.

Sixth, courageous deeds. Romero began to transfer priests who were unwilling to accept the idea of serving the people to posts where they could do no harm or, at least, where their countertestimony would not be so serious. For example, one priest who was the type who considered himself "faithful" and "good" decided to leave the diocese; he took refuge under the protective wing of the papal nuncio. We will refrain from naming names.

The church that we had planned in our weeks of pastoral studies was beginning to take shape. Even though it stayed on the drawing board for the majority, there was a minority who put the ideas into practice and who were stigmatized as subversives. And they were.

April 1977—First Pastoral Letter

Bishop Romero had a talent for communication. He had a reporter's instinct, and a real passion for the mass media. In the diocese of San Miguel he had his own newsletter and his own radio program. One of his few personal possessions was recording equipment for radio programs.

When he arrived in San Salvador he began to write a weekly column in the newspaper *Prensa Gráfica* and another in the archdiocesan weekly *Orientación,* and soon he began a radio program on the Catholic broadcasting station, YSAX. It had as its theme "Feeling with the Church," and took the form of a dialogue with the people. He never missed this program. Even when he was outside the country he would call the station and do the program by telephone.

He enjoyed writing letters. I think there must be hundreds of Christians in the countryside of El Salvador who have letters from Bishop Romero, because he answered every letter he received. And hundreds of *campesinos* and factory workers wrote him. An old woman in Honduras corresponded regularly with him.

And, to tell the truth, he was a good writer. In print, though, his discourse lacked some of the spice and humor that showed up in personal contacts: this, however, may have been due to the discipline of rationality and logical order that he imposed on himself.

When he became bishop of San Salvador, he decided to communicate in his role as bishop by means of pastoral letters. Two the first year, and once each year after that.

The first letter was an Easter message. Our bishop had had a deep experience of faith and persecution. The ruling powers had assassinated Rutilio Grande and expelled a significant group of well qualified pastoral workers. The bishop had gathered off the street of El Salvador the bodies of many dead activists and catechists from among the Christian communities . . . and he had begun to discover a renewed and powerful church.

The letter is quite churchy sounding, but a new, direct style comes through and a searching out for a new partner in dialogue: the people. He was not pessimistic: "If I were to look for an adjective to describe this time of change in the archdiocese, I would not hesitate to call it the hour of resurrection."

He felt that he was the successor to a great man, Bishop Luis Chávez, and that because of the maturity of the priests he could enter into a dialogue with them. The letter was a call to dialogue and reflection.

He also pointed to the seed of a new ecclesiology: "The church does not live for its own sake."

The letter, in fact, had little impact in the base communities. It seems strange to be reading it over again now, but it clearly shows his desire to make the church confront the future with hope. It was just one week before the assassination of Alfonso Navarro.

May 11, 1977—Alfonso Navarro, Martyr

Alfonso Navarro was ordained to the diocesan priesthood in 1967, and his sacerdotal ministry flowered in the atmosphere of Medellín—the "revolutionary" first general assembly of CELAM (*Conferencia Episcopal Latinoamericana,* Latin American Episcopal Conference). He was one of the founders of the new pastoral ministry with the *campesinos.* Weekend retreats and the training of catechists and lay ministers became more and more common all over Opico, where he was stationed. As the 1970s began, conflicts began to storm around him.

Then came the first kidnaping of someone from the Salvadoran ruling class: Regalado Dueñas. The kidnapers called themselves "The Group." Alfonso was accused of being their accomplice. He had to appear at an official investigation; Bishop Rivera accompanied him. As a result, Alfonso had to leave Opico. In the parish register he left his words of farewell and his signature:

I bid you all farewell, reminding you of the words of St. Paul that inspire my whole life as a priest: "The truth will make you free." And if you are killed because of it, may that death be welcome: resurrection will also come, because "he who looks after his life will lose it and he who loses his life for my sake will find it." Good-bye.

Alfonso Navarro, 1971.

He was transferred to an upper-class parish in the Miramonte section of the city of San Salvador. Parishioners there were accustomed to a "modern," urban pastoral methodology, with foreign borrowings. They were like a gringo parish in the midst of a Central American city. Alfonso had a different approach.

He tried to get along with them, but his efforts came to naught, one by one. Basic communities did not work out there. He turned to the youth, but it was at the time when General Medrano was introducing them to marihuana as a means of weakening the emerging revolutionary youth organizations. Bad times.

Miramonte is the "asphalt desert of the city of the rich." Alfonso had no other means than the Word, and he used it in his sermons. Then the persecution began; it brought him to the verge of a nervous collapse. The "good, rich" Catholics could not put up with the words of a prophet.

They moved on to deeds. On January 11 his car and garage were blown sky-high by a bomb; it was powerful enough to destroy his house as well. On February 28 he preached the sermon at the Mass in Plaza Libertad, showing himself to be at the heart of the people and their struggle. The death threats then became a daily occurrence.

When they finally killed Alfonso, Bishop Romero took his life to his own heart and with it challenged all of Salvadoran society. In a sermon he said, "Alfonso is like a Bedouin in the desert who says to travelers 'not that way, not that way,' but they pay no attention and they kill him."

Our bishop now knew that the ruling class was capable of anything. He began to discover the intrinsic evil of the economic system:

How evil this system must be to pit the poor against the poor, the peasant in army uniform against the worker peasant.

"If I were to look for an adjective to describe this time of change in the archdiocese, I would not hesitate to call it the hour of resurrection."

II

Education of a Bishop

For a number of years the priests of the archdiocese had been meeting frequently. Regular meetings were scheduled for every month and the agenda came from current events. Since 1977 the meetings became more frequent and grew in size as a result of the martyrdom of Rutilio Grande and Alfonso Navarro. And they had been enriched by the presence of the nuns who worked in the parish ministry and the base communities, and some of the lay leaders of these communities. Study weeks had often been the culmination of regional meetings aimed at studying and reorienting pastoral planning. All of this generated a tendency toward unification among the different sectors of the Salvadoran church.

There were also spiritual retreats. The archdiocese organized two or three each year. We were free to set them up as we wished as long as they responded to real needs.

In 1977 a group of us met beforehand to plan our retreat. We were all priests with a lot in common because of our similar pastoral work. We put our retreat plan on the bulletin board of the seminary. We felt the need to discuss among ourselves our commitment to the process as it appeared at that moment in history. Above all, we wanted to analyze and understand the times more clearly and see them in the perspective of the Father.

And the bishop landed in our midst! He saw the announcement and thought it would be a good opportunity to make a spiritual retreat. He did not notice the names of those who made up the group. We had major existential problems that we wanted to discuss, of course, and we were not following a plan of individual meditation or the traditional retreat format. We wanted to live the experience of Jesus, "discovering God's will through conflict and struggle" (Heb. 5:8).

During the first days Romero escaped from us to his accustomed solitude. That was his experience of God. But little by little he joined our common search, participated in our study sessions, and came into personal contact with all of us.

And on the last day he told us: "I had no idea of whom I was getting mixed up with; when I saw the group that first night, I was shocked. . . . I had really never experienced the depth of prayer that can exist in a group like this one, discussing and sharing its experiences in the presence of God."

And they truly were days of intense reflection. And we spoke quite clearly of our commitments. The bishop listened much of the time and with great respect. He still did not understand much of what we were doing or looking for. I believe that he gained a great deal of confidence in us. In fact his confidence was greater than his understanding or acceptance of our point of view. Because of this, he began to support us even at times when there was a great deal of opposition.

The Chancery Coffee Lounge

One day we found Bishop Romero moving everything out of the office where the photocopier had stood. "We're going to turn this into a coffee lounge." The silent man who had been used to making decisions all by himself was now keen on dialogue. And we had to soften the austere feeling of the chancery—a narrow hall with ten doors off it—in order to turn it into a place suitable for informal meetings, a center for communion.

Workers on strike, blue-eyed journalists with blond hair, lay ministers, *campesinos* hounded by the National Guard, seminarians, bishops, priests—they all used the chancery coffee lounge as a gathering place. "Meet me at the coffee lounge." The idea behind it was a brilliant inspiration.

Every morning it was a beehive of activity. Unlike chancery offices elsewhere, the San Salvador chancery began to have the atmosphere of a "home away from home." When priests from the small rural towns had a few spare minutes before catching a bus back, they would stop by the coffee lounge, knowing they would find interesting persons there and get caught up on the local news.

The church of San Salvador was becoming a church of communion, of participation. Bishop Chávez had brought it up to date in its collegial structure and the pastoral commission was alive, in constant touch with the grassroots. Bishop Romero strengthened it and fostered a dynamic of participation—but it was already walking on its own two feet, an adult church.

A ministry of solidarity and information started functioning in the chancery to serve the popular movements, church organizations, and the entire population. The Catholic radio station and the newspaper *Orientación* began to make an impressive impact. The impact was both ecclesial and political, both national and international. The coffee lounge played a role in all this.

The chancery was also home for the laity commission, the national pastoral council, other pastoral organizations and their lay representatives, with Bishop Romero at the center of things and always moving. You would see him in his office where the door was always open, in the hallway, or in the coffee lounge. Whether smiling or serious, he always mirrored the profound silence that seemed at his very core. Our bishop was a living presence, even when he was not there. He always left word where we could find him. When something unexpected came up, he would go out into the hall himself and call everyone together so that he could ask our advice. He spoke little and listened much; and when he spoke, it was from the silent wellspring within him—the sign of a man of prayer.

Upstairs was his room, his personal secretary's office, his small radio, recording equipment, and his books. There one could see the hundreds of letters from *campesinos* who wrote to him every day, the little coffee cups to help make it easier to talk things over and encourage familiarity. A small space, just enough for resting up a little or for meditation before making an important decision. There was also a minicoffee lounge for more private moments and relaxation.

May 19, 1977—Martyrdom of Aguilares

The *campesinos* organized in the Popular Revolutionary Bloc *(Bloque Popular Revolucionario*, BPR) had taken over some land in order to plant a crop.

First they had tried every legal way of getting work or a place to grow enough to survive; then through legal means they tried to get permission to rent some poor and unused plots of land at a price they could afford. It was useless. So they took over land with the intention of paying what rent they could—the San Francisco farm, near the village of El Paisnal, not far from the town of Aguilares.

The *campesinos* were about to see their crops come up. There had been days of intense work and preparation. Everything was shared; the work was organized communally, with evaluation discussions at night, along with technical and political training sessions. It was a whole new experience of life and community, of working, of learning, of worshiping together—but. . . .

The "uniformed beasts" arrived in Aguilares. They were poor peasants themselves, dressed up in army uniforms and defending interests not their own. They came in trains and trucks, and they attacked by air (parachutists) and land . . . and all they found were some dirty dishes. The security system of the BPR had worked and the villagers were back in their homes. The army officers thought that the ones they were especially looking for would be in the church with the priests.

The officers gave the signal for attack and the village was occupied. Two soldiers were stationed at the entrance of every house to prevent those inside from leaving their homes. The soldiers could not find the *campesinos* they were looking for. In the church they found only five priests and two villagers. One of the latter wanted to ring the bells to summon the people to defend the church; he was killed as he climbed the bell tower.

Every house was searched. Everyone found with a Bible or a parish songbook was taken prisoner. Many were beaten; some were killed.

The soldiers dragged out the four foreign Jesuits priests, beat them up, tortured them, and then drove them to the Guatemalan border and expelled them from El Salvador. Father Guevara, a Salvadoran national, was handcuffed and thrown into a truck jammed with arrested villagers. In jail he was tied to the cell bars between beatings.

When they overcame their fright, the three hundred jailed villagers managed to coordinate themselves; they sang songs of

Christian hope. When food was thrown at them as if they were pigs, they gathered it up in an orderly way and distributed it in equal portions. Their jailers were astonished. "We shall overcome."

Aguilares was occupied by the army for almost a month.

The church had been attacked from all four sides; everything in sight was destroyed. The tabernacle was emptied and the communion breads for the community were thrown on the floor.

It was a symbol of the total desecration of the Eucharist, the Body of Christ: the community, the people, the priests, the eucharistic bread—*all* smashed and annihilated on the road to liberation.

Again our bishop asked us to open our homes to the refugees, to that living, bleeding, terrorized Eucharist running and hiding in the city streets. Romero was deeply affected by this incident. We told him about the organization's leaders who met in our sacristies, and he asked us to care for them. All of this was new for him.

Aguilares has become a symbol. It has also earned a place in the poetry and song of the communities:

> Death has struck your face,
> land of courageous cane fields.
> Your name grows, Aguilares,
> with the blood of the dead.
> Your story was born simply,
> with the rhythm of hunger and patience,
> and the voice of your
> brave consciousness grew,
> winning the sun.
>
> But the beast grew
> and, in its hate, devoured you.
> Rifles and helmets rose up,
> filling your fields with fear and anger.
>
> Where can they be—Nelson, Rutilio, Manuel,
> and all the other innocent loved ones
> taken away by repression?

Someday your bells
will silence the guns.
Your voices in the wind
will end the torment,
and bring back harmony.

Blood was spilled again
and became a seed!
You will hear the voice of the prophet,
and the sound of warfare.
But your songs will be heard
above the roar of the cannon.
Your voices in the wind
will end the torment,
and bring back harmony.

June 1977—Learning from the People

Sunday was always a heavy workday for Bishop Romero. Besides saying the office with the nuns in the hospital and his own prayers, he had to be at the door of the cathedral for the entrance procession at 8:00 A.M. Mass lasted two hours, and then he would attend to the needs of the people filling the church: the old woman, the boy scout, the foreign reporter. . . . They wanted to greet him and he had an enormous patience that paid no attention to the criteria of what might be a "more efficient" use of time.

But one Sunday he had to leave the cathedral early. The National Guard had attacked a small village, and he wanted to go and share the life of his people. The town, Jicarón, is north of San Salvador, forty-three miles by car and then two and a half more on a muddy footpath. There he found the community joyfully singing: "Welcome, brothers in Christ, to hear the Word of God"—as if nothing had happened in the village. But their houses had been ransacked, their pigs and chickens killed, their supply of grain scattered over the ground.

It was late by then and the bishop asked for some food. All they gave him was a small tamale. But he was hungry and asked for something more. His requests went unanswered.

Later on, when he met for an evaluation with the seminarian, the nun, and the lay ministers of the community, he told them of his impression that something was wrong between himself and the people there because he had not been given enough to eat. They explained to him that the people had not given him anything because they had nothing to give; many of them had nothing at all to eat that whole day. Then Bishop Romero understood—and asked forgiveness.

The National Guard also killed a number of *campesinos* in Chalatenango, in the Arcatao region. It is a difficult journey, but the bishop went there and spoke to the people. They were upset with him. They asked him to make public the names of the assassins. They could hardly understand what for them were abstractions and roundabout expressions on his part, and they protested. They tried to take the microphone out of his hand.

Bishop Romero did not understand what was wrong. He had made every sacrifice he could for them. Later, someone in the chancery said that it was no way to treat such a good bishop. We found out what had happened and we explained it to him. Then he realized that when he denounced something in the name of the poor he had to be concrete and direct.

Widows and Orphans . . .

Some friends of Juancito came to my house. They had to find him. (Juancito is Juan Chacón, who later became secretary general of the BPR.) The Federal Police and National Guard had just killed Juancito's father, Don Chus.

Don Chus (Felipe de Jesús) was a cursillo member, a lay minister in his parish church, and a coordinator of basic communities around Tejutla. He had had problems with the local pastor, an Italian priest with fascistic leanings, but Don Chus believed he had to continue supporting the church. He was loved by all, and had a beautiful family. He understood his son's militancy; he came to me and told me about his son, and we spoke of how we could help him. He was a good man, a good father, Christian to the core.

I told all this to Bishop Romero, who had not known Don Chus very well. He asked me to go to see the family in his name; he could not go at that moment but he would later. And he asked me to tell him more about the Christians who belonged to Marxist organizations—country workers and factory workers.

On the ninth day after the death of Don Chus, Bishop Romero told me he wanted to go with me to El Salitre, where the family lived, to be with them and to preach about hope in the midst of death. Evangelina, the widow, was happy to receive the bishop in her home. Later we all went to the nearby chapel, still under construction.

"These days I have to walk the roads gathering up dead friends, listening to widows and orphans, and trying to spread hope." Those were the opening words of his sermon in the chapel, so small that we barely fit in.

In the chancery the next day we spoke about how incredible that rural family was—the strength of the mother, Evangelina, serving us tamales and fruit juice after her husband's novena and telling us how they had found him drawn and quartered, unrecognizable, with dogs eating at him.

An Evening with the Bishop

Bishop Romero kept asking about the participation of Christians in political activities, about the crisis of faith that it entailed, and the transformation of values. He listened, in silence. He listened and I realized that it still did not fit into his conceptual framework but that he had a great respect for the people and wanted to understand them. Bishop Romero always wagered on the side of the people.

One night I was at a meeting of a group of mostly young Christian activists. The discussion had come to a standstill, and someone suggested, "Why don't we go talk to the bishop? Maybe he's alone and we can get to know him better." And we headed out, walking down the streets of Miramonte toward the little cancer hospital run by the Carmelite nuns where he lived.

He greeted us, pleased to see us and evidently revitalized by our presence. It was 9:30 P.M. Joaquín played the guitar and Bishop Romero joined us in singing songs of hope and struggle. Then a few funny and earthy ones, plus love ballads . . . the guitar lends itself to all kinds of moods.

Suddenly the bishop began to talk confidentially to us about his problems. The papal nuncio was openly performing religious ceremonies for government officials, saying Mass for them in the nunciature. And some priests were causing a negative influence, and he had had to remove them from their parishes because they were not doing their duty. (We would call them "reactionary," but the bishop did not use this term.)

The group was even more surprised when he said, "I'd like to hear the opinion of the young people on our problem with the nunciature."

Joaquín put the guitar down in the corner, and Tomás looked at me with his mouth wide open. Yolanda made the first move and asked, "Could you describe more concretely what the problem is?"

As Bishop Romero talked, he said things that astonished us, and as he continued our astonishment increased. He had been named bishop because they wanted someone who would put the Marxist priests and the base communities in their place and would improve relations with the government, because they had deteriorated under our previous bishop, Luis Chávez.

Bishop Romero was very impressed by the maturity of those young Christians. When the group left the hospital, we found a place where we could all sit down on the ground, as if we had just reached the top of a mountain without quite believing it and had to wait a few minutes to really grasp it. At that moment someone said, "We've got to help that man."

And help him they did—with their whole hearts—for three years.

I could tell a thousand more stories like this one. And there is something that all of them would show: Bishop Romero was in a dialectical—a give-and-take—relationship with the people, learning the true meaning of reality and the prophetic lessons of the gospel from them.

Up to the last moment of his life he adhered to this learning process—a permanent attitude of search and of fidelity.

The base communities in El Salvador, even as they continue to battle while suffering the birth pangs of a rejuvenated Christianity, are writing down and gathering together all the "educational-liberating" moments they had with Bishop Romero—or, as we often called him, "the old man" or "uncle," his clandestine name in the communities.

July 1, 1977—Presidential Inauguration, Episcopal Abstention

The new president of the republic took office. He came from the heart of the repressive forces that have dominated our country since 1932.

He became president as the result of electoral fraud that was more blatant than ever before. I remember Luis and Pepe that night when they knocked on my door; they were in tears. They had been counting votes when the National Guard arrived, beat them up, knocked over the ballot box, and took it with them.

During the last few days before the inauguration, the new president had sent messages to Archbishop Romero inviting him to the inaugural ceremony. The president had made many promises and applied pressure through the papal nuncio, other bishops, and friends. But our bishop saw clearly what he was up to and did not give in. The preconditions set for church-state dialogue had not changed: an end to the repression of the people, an explanation of the assassinations of priests and catechists, and the return of deported priests. *Then* there could be talk about a dialogue.

In a meeting held at that time, a progressive priest suggested the possibility of giving dialogue a try. Bishop Romero, breaking his silence on the matter, said, "They just want to flirt, not change. We don't need government power to spread the gospel."

And he did not go. That presidential inauguration was condemned by the people. The bishop's absence was conspicuous.

The solution to national problems suggested by the president, General Carlos H. Romero, was ridiculous and cynical. "We shall ask the rich to give more to the poor, and ask the poor to express their thankfulness."

August 1977—Second Pastoral Letter

The experience of the base communities and the political crisis that the country was going through had shaken many concepts of the church and the pastoral ministry. We had to rethink our ecclesiology to be able to respond to the new challenges. After two weeks of pastoral meetings, the church of San Salvador had matured a great deal, and we felt the need to gather together and share our experiences and thoughts. That is how the second pastoral letter was born. I sincerely believe that the letter also represented a personal effort by the bishop to renew his own theology.

The result, however, was a very doctrinal piece of writing. One can see in it the gentle but razor-sharp influence of Jesuit Jon Sobrino, who would be of such great help in the whole process of theological development by the bishop and the Salvadoran church. At any rate, the copy I now have was lent to me by one of the nuns who would later break with the traditional role of the Catholic schools and go out to do direct pastoral work with the rural poor. On the first page of the letter she wrote: "Here's material for study classes."

In it Romero insisted that the church is not an end in itself and that the trial we were living through "has deepened the church's consciousness in two major ways: in the sense it has of its presence in the world and in its service to the world."

We do not want a church that is on the sidelines of the historical process. Following Christ makes the church dynamic, and choosing the cause of the poor gives the church its true point of view. Our "church has become profoundly aware of the relationship that exists between the history of a people and the history of salvation."

There was something new in the way he treated the subject of Marxism. He considered it a complex problem, "which one must study from the economic, scientific, political, philosophical, and religious viewpoints, and from the viewpoint of one's own historical situation." Only an "ideology of atheism" (in other words, metaphysical materialism) is incompatible with the Christian faith.

He also gave new life to the concept of "church unity," which can be reached only through "fidelity to the Word and the demands of Jesus Christ. It is based on shared suffering. There can be no church unity if we ignore the world in which we live."

This second pastoral letter is very important, but it did not go so far as the actual practice we had embraced by that time in the ecclesial communities at the local level.

The Bishop's Sunday Sermons

I know someone who worked for a company that calculated the size of various audiences for advertising agencies. She dug up confirmed figures for radio audiences in El Salvador. The first finding was that the bishop's Sunday sermon had by far the largest audience of any program in the country. The figures are quite clear. His audience was 73 percent of the countryside and 47 percent of urban areas—and the sermons lasted at least an hour and a half.

It was the time when our bishop's voice could be heard coming from houses, cars, and the transistor radios of persons walking down the street. But not everyone felt safe turning the volume up. A friend told me that soon after Bishop Romero's sermons started, the sale of earphones in his store doubled. The *campesinos*, especially, were aware that it might be dangerous to be known as someone who listened to Bishop Romero on the radio.

But something that not everyone knows is that the bishop's sermons were not the work of just one man speaking courageously about the liberating gospel, but the work of an entire church backing up its bishop and helping him compose each Sunday sermon. Helpers ranged from René, who organized the information that came in and clipped out newspaper articles every day, to the communities that sent in their accusations and recounted their lives of conflict. Others wrote up a summary of the events of the week from the chancery legal aid office that passed on news about the legal battles to force the government to tell families where their "disappeared" relatives were, about prisoners, labor problems, and the latest killings. There were the clandestine messengers, who always seemed to arrive at the cathedral at the very last minute to tell us what had just happened. And there were others. We all wrote the bishop's Sunday sermon, and he was never more a bishop than when he gathered all that information together and electrified it with the gospel for the poor. . . making it the sermon for the day.

Many persons have said that they would like to publish all of his sermons. It would probably be impossible: many of them no longer exist in written form or could be found only on a tape made while someone was listening at home; maybe some fragments could still be found unerased at YSAX. Perhaps most of them could be found at the radio station and be published. But the life that those sermons reflect can be found only in the people who lived them.

The sermons could also be studied to show how the bishop became more and more aware in his understanding and his preaching of the importance of the life of the people, and how he reread the gospel in a historical context and from the new point of view he was gradually adopting.

We must today find new ways to evangelize; Bishop Romero's sermons reveal his awareness of this duty. We must proclaim—for all the world to hear—the truth about the people's lives and their organizations. We must condemn the reaction—that is, repression—that exploiters resort to in order to block advances made by the people. We must participate in the activities of the base communities within this historical process. We must discover, from within this context, the evangelical values alive in all this. We must preach the Word of God as hope for the poor.

This would be a kind of general outline. To understand how Bishop Romero gave it life you really have to put yourself in his cathedral, packed with the poor, and the amazed reporters who had heard what was happening there but had never imagined it could be what it was. The crowd reached all the way to the altar; those in front were touching it. Many brought snacks with them and sat on the floor.

I shall never forget the expressions on the faces of those elegant Jesuit priests—professors from Georgetown University, the distinguished institution of higher learning in Washington, D.C.—who came to the cathedral on February 14, 1978, to present Bishop Romero with an honorary Ph.D. They, the bishop, and invited guests were literally forced against the wall by the crowd. The expressions on their faces revealed their utter lack of understanding of what was going on, plus the fear of being crushed. Some of the old women who had brought flowers for Bishop Romero decided to leave them at the feet of the frightened foreign dignitaries. Romero just smiled.

In El Salvador, the Word of God can no longer be imprisoned in sterile orthodoxies or corseted with ahistorical moralism. The

Word of God is like a caged dove that has regained its freedom and flies off taking with it the great news of the liberation of the oppressed.

An Auxiliary Bishop

Bishop Romero's option on the side of the poor brought him into conflict, sometimes very painful, with many who had earlier been his friends and who, with the best of intentions, had chosen a different course to pursue.

This was the case with his auxiliary bishop, René Revelo. When Romero was named archbishop in February 1977, he asked for a trustworthy auxiliary bishop and remembered his friend Revelo, who was at that time auxiliary bishop in the Santa Ana diocese. But changes took place very quickly, and the distance between them suddenly widened.

The break between Romero and the Salvadoran episcopal conference turned into a festering wound. This was especially hard for him because he had dedicated a large part of his life to the "institutional church." His motto was "Feel with the Church." As episcopal secretary for many years in the diocese of San Miguel, he often had to cover up the deficiencies of the bishop in order to maintain a more or less unsullied image of the church. This conflict between his basic personal honesty and his loyalty to the institutional church created tensions that nearly tore him apart internally. The theological framework he had learned in the 1940s at the Gregorian University in Rome gave him no alternative.

Dedication and loyalty were what made Romero, from certain points of view, the perfect candidate to be archbishop of San Salvador. He was "safe" in doctrine and in his personal life, he was familiar with the ecclesiastical jungle, he made strong decisions and would be able to reroute the militant church of San Salvador that was heading down the revolutionary path of the Salvadoran people. But as it turned out, he chose the side of the poor.

Nine months later, when the auxiliary was officially named, Romero and all of us felt threatened. Bishop Revelo had taken part in an investigation of the "orthodoxy" of the priests of the people's church and accused us of being subversives. He had been sent to the Bishops Synod in Rome that same year and publicly, both at the synod and to the international press, had labeled our group of priests Marxists. The lay ministers and catechists in our communities he labeled Maoists. When Bishop Romero heard the news he did not want to believe it and called Rome to find out for sure. The report was confirmed. It provoked a deluge of protests.

Nonetheless, before Bishop Revelo arrived in San Salvador, Bishop Romero talked to a number of Revelo's priest friends, assigned him to one of the best parishes in downtown San Salvador, and gave him the post of vicar general of the diocese. But Revelo never attended the monthly meetings of the priests of the diocese and did not even go to the pastoral planning sessions for his own vicariate.

Then an irreversible conflict arose. Caritas, the interdiocesan organization that distributes development aid to local communities, was being manipulated by government ministries and the military to try to win the popularity they lacked among the people. In other words, Caritas was being used against the people. Bishop Romero placed in charge of it a priest who was very committed to the poor. He began to uncover the whole mess as he tried to make sure that funds were channeled to development projects. Because of all this the episcopal conference tried to take away Bishop Romero's place on the national Caritas board and give it to the president of the episcopal conference. To do this, they took advantage of Romero's absence from the country and, conniving with the government, they used Auxiliary Bishop Revelo to carry out the change, despite the fact that Revelo knew he did not have the archbishop's approval. He did, however, have the government's approval.

After a great deal of consultation, Bishop Romero suspended his auxiliary bishop as vicar general and announced the suspension in a sermon and in the archdiocesan newspaper, *Orientación*. And he stuck to his decision despite pressure from the papal nunciature.

This was but one more incident that added to the distance between the bishops. Romero's evangelical radicalism allowed him no other choice. Nor was he alone. He was acting within a church that was pledged to commitment and service to those who resisted the machinations of the powerful.

Moreover, it was not the first time that faith in the gospel had created this kind of problem. The Salvadoran church has often had to face up to moments of evangelical truth.

1978—Third Pastoral Letter

The Church and Popular Political Organizations

At last!—a pastoral letter dealing with a subject of conflict and urgency, a subject that the communities had dealt with and on which they had come to a practical agreement, namely, the popular political organizations. In a meeting of the priests who belonged to the Pastoral Reflection Group, we had analyzed the problem and arrived at a course of action we had been following for a number of years. Evidently it was a problem that was also bothering Rome: the bishops of El Salvador were instructed to make their position clear.

On the other hand, this problem was also worrying the revolutionary organizations. In 1975 the People's Liberation Forces (FPL) had sent a letter to all the progressive priests acknowledging their work in the conscientization of the people and mentioning their respect for those who were faithful to their beliefs and to the gospel, and asking all of them to collaborate in the process of liberating the poor of our country.

The FPL's letter brought the problem and the conflict out into the open. The bishops of Santa Ana, San Vicente, and San Miguel, resorting to old papal encyclicals, took advantage of the occasion to condemn the popular organizations as "materialistic" and "atheistic." The fragile shell of bureaucratic unity was shattered.

It was a subject that had tremendous political repercussions. The regions where the popular organizations flourished were the same ones where the gospel of liberation had been preached. The Christian communities had grown in their understanding of the ways of practical love, of political interpretations of faith, and they now identified the oppressive system as the enemy of life and, therefore, as contrary to the kingdom of God.

Those were days when the poor took to the streets in the struggle for their most basic demands—their immediate needs and their long-term goal: the formation of a new society of freedom, sharing, and community.

The interpretation of the Salvadoran upper class was simple and specious: "The peasants have been subverted by the propaganda of the Marxist clergy."

A panel discussion was held on the subject at the University of Central America (UCA). Bishop Romero was seated at the conference table with Polin (Apolinario Serrano), who at the time was secretary general of the rural workers who belonged to the Popular Revolutionary Bloc. Someone asked him, "Isn't it true that all this trouble was started by the priests?" His answer was devastatingly clear: "The trouble was started by the reality of our everyday life. When we come home after working like dogs in the hot sun and don't even have enough money to buy medicine for a sick child, we have to do something. So what do you think causes us to act?" At this response the bishop laughed and joined in the long applause. . . .

Polin, together with Patricia Huertas, Félix García, and José López, was later murdered by the military dictatorship. The Salvadoran people venerate him as a great Christian leader and martyr.

The relationship between the workers' organizations and the church had always been fruitful. It should not be forgotten that in the great popular insurrection of 1932 the Christian confraternities played an important role.

By this time the fourteen families that make up the Salvadoran oligarchy blamed everything on the church. And their version of the country's problems was the one that got to Rome. The Salvadoran upper-class Catholics wanted to condemn the church to death: they were the ones who spread flyers and painted slogans all over San Salvador: "Be patriotic: kill a priest." And they believed that the BPR, which at that time had more than eighty thousand members, was the political arm of our Christian base communities.

To frame an answer to the accusations, Bishop Romero summoned all of us to help him: the base communities, to tell him of our experiences; the theologians, to analyze and write about what we were doing; the lawyers from the chancery's legal aid office, to clear the legal hurdles. It was a joint undertaking that brought us into a new kind of communication and ecclesial dialogue.

In his resultant pastoral letter our bishop no longer spoke as someone who felt that he had the whole truth in his possession, nor did he sit in judgment on the situation; rather, he acted as a pastor. He told us that "our limitations demand that this be a dialogue." He began with an analysis of the populist political organizations, what they had undertaken, and the violent repression they suffered. He laid out the challenges that this implied for the church and he spoke of the give-and-take relationship that should exist between the popular organizations and the base communities. The letter did not reflect a proud dogmatism; it was a plea for a joint search.

He had asked those of us who represented the base communities to develop a questionnaire to be sent out with the pastoral letter, to facilitate study in local communities, neighborhoods, and parishes. He asked us to report on the results of our reflections so that we could continue to elaborate a vision of faith that would strengthen the people in its march toward freedom and strengthen the church in its fidelity to its obligations.

Perhaps the point of greatest conflict in all of this was the issue of violence. Although a qualitative advance was made in dealing with the subject, the pastoral letter did not make a clear distinction between brute terrorism, which must always be condemned, and revolutionary violence.

What the people saw in all of this was that Bishop Romero had taken the side of the masses and their organizations. That was our bishop!

Andrés Torres

It would have been wonderful to have seen Andrés Torres (Antonio, in the FPL) reading that pastoral letter in the mountains of Chalatenango. But he died before the letter was issued.

Born in Apaneca, he had grown up under the wing of Father Cea. He always found some free time from work and his organizational responsibilities to spend in prayer. He lived his faith in the Masses celebrated in the *campesino* villages. He helped with training courses in their communities; his favorite theme was "national reality." He struck sparks in many minds. *Campesinos* said of him that "he made things clear to us."

He died a hero's death in Santa Tecla, with Eva (Clara Elizabeth Ramírez de Solano) and Francisco (José Alejandro Solano). Caught in a house surrounded by government forces, they were killed in a shoot-out that lasted nine hours. They chose to fight to the death rather than allow themselves to be taken prisoners. With his own blood, Antonio wrote the letters FPL on the wall.

There were to be other "Antonios" to trek the road of Salvadoran liberation who would be thankful to our bishop for the gift of his pastoral letter and for his courage.

A New Impetus for Church Unity

One day a group of young men came to the chancery meeting room. They told me they were from the First Emmanuel Church. They were Baptists who wanted to start a dialogue with us.

They told us their story. They, and some representatives of other churches, had been called to a meeting at the president's house for a dialogue with the government, but no Catholics were invited. The government offered to help them with their "mission."

The Baptists refused to accept money themselves, but other Protestant colleagues agreed to the offer. Government officials told them that money that had been given to Catholics would now be given to them. The Baptists refused this kiss of Judas. They wanted to work with the persecuted Catholic church in order to be on the side of the poor in El Salvador.

I had never been in a dialogue with fundamentalists before, and something about the way they talked—the roundabout way they got at the world's problems through the Bible—seemed quite strange to me. But there they were, discovering a new way to forge unity among the churches. And there was not a trace of sectarianism or proselytizing.

As time went on, we kept our contacts and we started to work together. Church unity weeks were planned and shared together. Through things like that we got to know each other better and better.

Psychological Warfare

Edmundo, the coordinator of our base community, was the victim of a barbaric arrest in his own house. They found a copy of the Bible in his room and a wall poster that read: "Come, Lord, socialism isn't enough." That was his crime.

"You're one of those church people, right? We knew all along you were a subversive. You have to come with us."

Nights and days of questioning. "I belong to a Christian community. We just read the Bible and talk about it; we teach catechism." At last they let him go after a fine with which we are all too familiar: 30 colons, collected from among his friends.

He told us what had happened. They kept repeating the same line over and over again: "Don't be stupid. The bishop is paid by the communists and is laughing behind your backs. He sleeps with the nuns, has fancy cars, and we have documented proof of all the money they send him from foreign countries."

We all received anonymous letters telling us that we had fifteen days to get out of the country—or else! And daily telephone calls, and visits from men pretending to be drunk; they insulted and threatened us. Our meetings were always watched, and "friends" told us it would be best if we left the country.

"I am a shepherd who, with his people, has begun to learn a beautiful and difficult truth: our Christian faith requires that we submerge ourselves in the world."

"A bishop will die, but the church of God, which is the people, will never perish."

III

Crossfire

ANEP is the National Association of Private Enterprise *(Asociación Nacional de la Empresa Privada)* in El Salvador. It represents all the elements of the upper class: landowners, import-export entrepreneurs, financiers, and industrialists. It is the organization that provides unity among the capitalists and serves the interests of imperialism in the area. It is cohesive and dynamic. There have been times when it has directed the flow of capital in all of Central America. It controls the mass media and knows how to use them to its own advantage. When it decides to move, it can cause an economic boom or destroy whomever dares to stand in its way.

The powers of ANEP decided to move on Bishop Romero. A million-dollar advertising campaign was orchestrated against him. Some days the city seemed to be inundated with pamphlets against him, studded with sickening caricatures. They had their team of theologians whose writings appeared frequently in the newspapers. They dreamed up names for imaginary Catholic women's associations, trying to invoke the sacred principles of religion to get a crusade of faith going against Bishop Romero and the revolutionary church.

Then they started a new newspaper, *Opinión,* dedicated to character assassination and refutation of the bishop's sermons. They also attacked all of us who were in any way involved in his pastoral work. Fortunately, the Salvadoran clergy lived very upright lives; they did not offer an easy target for the attempts at scandalmongering. All this effort was financed by voluntary contributions from private enterprise. When they asked for money, their unscrupulous sales pitch was, "Give, so we can stop the bishop."

For a long time they thought they could get rid of Bishop Romero by driving him to a nervous breakdown. They knew that in times past the bishop had been obliged to go to Mexico for periods of rest. But now the bishop was whole, strong, sure of himself and sure of his mission.

The next strategy was to get at him through Rome. They named a special ambassador to the Holy See, one of the coffee barons from the city of Santiago de María, benefactor of the church and good friend of the reactionary bishops, Mr. Llach. The Roman Curia was soon flooded with rumors about the bishop. When he arrived for visits with the pope, the litany of accusations began: one priest smoked cigarettes during Mass, another celebrated Mass with coffee and sweet rolls, others were Marxists who committed the horrible sin of "getting involved in party politics."

And then the death threats: the car with unidentified gunmen who shot at his house, the anonymous phone calls, the letters. Later, the suitcase filled with dynamite left next to the place where he was about to celebrate Mass.

And the comings and goings of the "apostolic visitors" called in to examine his orthodoxy. Two of those official visitors in just three years had to be a world's record, to say nothing of the "unofficial" visit of the papal nuncio from Costa Rica.

The internal pressures were also intense and even more hurtful, because of the kind of churchman he was.

Caught in a crossfire, he sometimes talked it over with us. He exacted from us a promise not to create unnecessary or artificial problems, but not to be afraid to do what had to be done about real problems.

November 28, 1978—Ernesto Barrera, Guerrilla-Priest

Ernesto (Neto) Barrera was a member of the People's Liberation Forces (FPL) and pastor of St. Sebastian's in Ciudad Delgado. We had heard about Fathers Camilo Torres, Pedro Laín, Gaspar García Laviana, and others, who had been killed while participating in armed revolutionary struggles, but they had left their pastoral work before joining the guerrillas.

That day, at noon, the word spread from mouth to mouth through the halls of the chancery, "They have killed Neto in a shoot-out with the guerrillas."

The first priest that I ran into said, "And now what do we do?" That short phrase, when fully spelled out, meant something like this: "What happened to the murdered priests Rutilio Grande and Alfonso Navarro was all right, but now we'll have no way of defending a church that held within it a man like Neto, who turns out to be a 'terrorist.' "

Another priest told me with even more cruelty, "The rumor at the beginning was that it was you, but I knew it wasn't true because you're not that stupid. . . ." The only friend of Neto's I could find there was Father Xavier.

At that moment the bishop called us all together with the usual question: "I need your advice. What should we do?" The meeting was on the second floor, in the bishop's small office. And this time we had to face it head on. No way to call it anything else—the issue was "revolutionary violence."

Until that day the bishop had maintained the easy posture of condemning all violence no matter what its origin. In his third pastoral letter he had made distinctions but had never really grappled with the problem of revolutionary violence.

We had already had vigorous discussions about it the previous year during a study week for priests of the archdiocese. However, it was a subject that was usually avoided.

Our bishop was feeling intense sorrow. Some months earlier he had entrusted Neto and me with being sure that there was a Christian presence in the union movement. He did this in spite of those who had told him not to trust us; he gambled on Neto's integrity.

It was very difficult to talk that afternoon. The opinions of the majority were very negative. Father Marcos, for example, told him, "Hand over the corpse to the family and let them bury him alone in the little village where he came from. . . ." Everyone had a different opinion.

Finally Xavier spoke. He was very moved and his eyes were filled with tears, "Look, bishop, we aren't sure how Neto died, but we do know one thing for certain: if Neto died with a gun in his hand, it wasn't to defend any kind of personal or selfish interest. He died because he was moved by his faith in the Lord and by his love for the people. He died fighting for the ideals of the poor, of the oppressed, of the exploited, fighting the cause of the poor. So I think the least we can do as a church is to give him a Christian burial as a priest of the church."

I had first met Neto in the 1960s, during the glory days of the Young Christian Workers. He was a seminarian then and felt crushed by the worker experience and the weight of secularization and violence it entailed. He had doubts about his vocation and difficulties with his studies because of all the time-consuming responsibilities he took on. When to study? Then came the conflict at the seminary as it took a turn to the right, just before his ordination. After that his whole life unfolded in the harsh world of the poor and the workers' movement, first in the suburban parish of Mejicanos and then in the parish of St. Sebastián in Ciudad Delgado.

When we had all spoken, the bishop surprised us with a question. He was pursuing a line of reasoning completely different from ours. "Don't you think that Neto's mother, without questioning the circumstances, will be next to the body of her son at the funeral? I, as his bishop, must be there also."

Once again our bishop had situated himself in the world of real persons and down-to-earth honesty. He still held to his earlier wager. He had opted for Neto during his lifetime, and now, in death, his decision was based on something beyond cold and calculating logic. He would be with him tomorrow at the funeral.

As we left the meeting I said "thank you" to him in a low voice.

And the pressure began. He had to play his cards very carefully now, but, no matter what, we would all be together tomorrow in the Eucharist, in the midst of the people, the ultimate victims of violence.

It hurt us that we could not carry Neto's body through the streets as we had Rutilio's. We ached because we could not bury him with his comrades who fell in the same struggle and with the same love, just as we had buried Luisito with Alfonso Navarro in the same grave. However, the important thing was that the bishop accepted Neto as a priest of the church and showed it by being present in the midst of the base communities on the day he was buried.

Those were very painful times. Some intellectuals who called themselves Christians could not understand someone like Neto and, out of a twisted notion of defending the church, they used the diocesan radio station to condemn him. They compared him to a rotten apple that had been removed from the basket in time to prevent the rest of the apples from going bad. Of course those intellectuals were speaking publicly to their secret audience, the middle-class groups who filled their classrooms and to whom they were beholden.

The internal crisis was so profound that when doubts started to surface about the truth of what had happened and it was being said that Neto had not died in a shoot-out, we encouraged that erroneous version ourselves because even many of us were not prepared to accept the facts. But at the same time we sent out a short study, "Violence, the Priest, and Politics," to all the base communities. It helped reflection and commitment a great deal, and it scandalized those who did not view the liberation process from the side of the poor.

The day before the death of Neto ("Monkey," as we affectionately called him, or "Felipe," his name in the FPL) we had had a meeting of the National Pastoral Group. Neto was especially restless and full of energy. He told us that it was extremely urgent that everything should be well organized among us. It was time to move on to more concrete activities.

Later we were having supper in an inexpensive restaurant and he again brought up the question we had asked ourselves over and over: what could we do so that the members of our communities could maintain their identity as Christians in the midst of the struggle and be able to explain to themselves and to others what they were doing? And, as always, we came up with the same answer, which we had to continue putting into practice in order to make it real: the mission of pastoral presence—maintaining an evangelical presence with Christians who had taken a radical political option in accordance with their consciences.

He was now present to all of us by the testimony of the life he had offered in sacrifice.

The following day we buried Valentín, Isidro, and Rafael— Neto's comrades-in-arms in the leadership of the revolutionary workers' movement and also in death. Only three priests came to that funeral. The three of us had to speak of hope to a battered, suffering working class. We had to confront a church that had not yet come to view things from the side of the poor.

When we went to the cemetery, the National Guard was waiting for us with guns raised. They had the whole cemetery surrounded. It was decided that only the women should go in with the bodies and bury them, to avoid further bloodshed. And so it was that the women—country workers, city workers, and students—buried our martyrs. At the end they had to flee because the "beasts" entered the cemetery and started to beat them with nightsticks.

Bishop Romero did not let us down. I can give personal testimony to that fact. Days before, Neto had planned a meeting of labor leaders with the bishop, to begin an open and frank dialogue. Bishop Romero now asked me to get together Neto's best friends from the revolutionary union movement so that we could take up the postponed dialogue. He invited us to his own residence, and we went. They came from the major companies: IMSA, El León (textiles), Gloves, S.A., CONELCA (electrical), and the like. We almost did not fit in the little room that the nuns had agreed the bishop could use for the meeting.

Neto's friends began to share their thoughts about him, and his stature grew in the eyes of the bishop. The personal and intimate problems that he had helped solve, the help they asked for, the encouragement he gave, the fearlessness that he imparted in the struggle . . . the clarity, the love, the concern with fidelity. Carmen, Rosario, Manolo . . . they were painting an image of Neto that many of his brother priests would never be able to understand because they were blinded by the traumatizing taboo on violence.

Those workers were genuinely surprised when the bishop said to them, "We must find someone who can take Neto's place and help you as he did." It was a moment of profound emotion for all of us. He asked them to suggest names. The person should be a Salvadoran who had not gotten into too much trouble already and who could identify deeply with the struggle of the people. He then added, "I'd like to continue this dialogue. How would you feel about meeting all afternoon on the day we celebrate the thirtieth-day memorial of Neto's death? We can get together in the Domus Mariae retreat house with you and some other workers, to see how we can continue moving forward together, and from there we can go to Neto's memorial Mass at Mejicanos." Bishop Romero was always surprising us. None of this had been planned in advance.

The FPL Letter

Bishop Romero had made public his doubts about the facts of Neto's participation in guerrilla activities, as well as the circumstances surrounding his death. This was a blow to the credibility of the information put out by the FPL. Because of this situation, FPL leaders wrote a long letter to Bishop Romero in which they explained Neto's active membership, his participation, his example, and the organization's respect for his Christian faith.

They also spoke of Christian participation in the revolutionary process in general. They explained to the bishop when and how the organization publicly acknowledged its active members. With all respect, they asked him to believe them.

Letters from the Base Communities

On the occasion of Neto's death various base communities likewise made public statements. For example:

- "We are all involved in a violent situation; the only question is, which side are you on?"
- "As Christians who love the church and who are committed to it, it hurts us to see that rich priests who use the sacraments to make money, who are distant from the people, and collaborate with the ruling class, are viewed as good persons, whereas poor priests, who are honest and committed to the poor, are labeled sinners. A sign hangs over their heads saying 'he gets involved in politics,' like the INRI that hung over the head of Jesus when they nailed him to the cross."
- "Whatever Neto's political choice was, we believe in him and are proud that he is our brother in the faith. We consider his testimony of the gospel as exemplary. Moved by faith, hope, and love, he gave his life, in God's name, for the people. He announced the Good News to the poor."
- "We are subjected to an incredibly expensive publicity campaign to convince us that any kind of armed struggle by the people

is terrorism. This kind of propaganda has led to the simplistic response of condemning all violence. It's necessary to clear the air of this kind of poison in order to be able to see clearly."

The Bishop and the Labor Movement

When Bishop Romero first arrived in San Salvador, a revitalization in the union movement had already begun. For years there had been virtually no activity in the labor movement. Its leadership had guided it into a purely economic struggle for higher wages, with no revolutionary goals. It had operated within a bourgeois legal framework and did not know how to combine the various means of struggle. Since the labor problems in Aceros, S.A. (steel), and the teacher strikes in the 1960s, nothing had been heard of militant workers or their struggles. The workers in our base communities who wanted to get involved in labor unions were always disappointed and frustrated by the bureaucracy in the unions.

Revolutionary mass organizations had emerged as early as 1974, but labor had not yet decided to join forces with them.

It was around 1976 when we started to hear about "the labor sector of the Popular Revolutionary Bloc" (BPR). They started out as an almost clandestine organization, because the owners knew the BPR only too well from its activities on their farms and coffee plantations. If they had known what was going on, they would have crushed it. We also began to hear of a new acronym that came from the eastern part of the country—COSDO *(Consejo Sindical de Oriente,* Eastern Labor Union Council).

Things were also heating up closer to home. From our own community there was Francisco, who was involved in forming a revolutionary nucleus in his section of the IMSA company; he brought us some new pamphlets. Juan Chacón told us about what he had been doing in the cardboard factory where he worked. But he was soon fired. Then there was the strike at El León textile company.

We realized that a slow but powerful movement had been going on. Organizing for the strike, the textile workers were able to restructure their union. Weaknesses of the previous leadership were avoided, and everything started to change. It was a difficult struggle. The company, which belongs to the Gadala María family, could hold out because it had a similar plant in San Cristóbal, in the Dominican Republic; that plant began to operate around the clock. But eventually the Salvadoran workers triumphed.

It was a totally new kind of strike. There was a vibrant feeling of self-assertiveness and proletarian joy: factory workers, *campesinos,* students . . . all working together. Rosita, a social worker, prepared lunches inside the factory building occupied by the union. An old man was singing and explaining his music to groups of workers. Another group would be gathered around an improvised blackboard, hearing about the philosophy of revolutionary labor unionization.

Pati, a student, arrived from completing her first turn on guard duty. "Hey, it was the first time I've felt what life and death are. I'll never know if I would have been able to do it, but when the police car came around the corner the second time, I had the Molotov cocktail ready in my hand."

Soon there was a convergence of the struggles that were being carried out by the landworkers, with their platform of better pay from the coffee, cotton, and sugar harvests, and the factory workers at INSA and El León. All of these groups belonged to the BPR. They decided to occupy the labor ministry. When the time came for mediation, the "Christian bosses" were pleased that the workers chose Bishop Romero as mediator. But Romero asked for political, juridical, and labor consultants, and named his own representative. It turned out to be an excellent piece of mediation. From then on he drew closer to the realities of the workers' world.

That was the public birth of the revolutionary labor movement. The repercussions were felt in the entire labor movement, which was in a seriously weakened position because of the history of repression. Only 30 percent of the nation's workers were organized and a good part of that percentage was manipulated by the government, the bourgeoisie, and imperialism through servile labor confederations with U.S. funding. Much of what remained of the labor movement was immobilized by legal machinery that had nothing to do with the interests of the majority. But then the whole union movement was shaken up and began to stand on its own feet, invigorated by the new winds of struggle and hope.

Because of all this, union leaders from groups such as CUTS (*Confederación Unitaria de Trabajadores Salvadoreños,* Unified Salvadoran Workers' Confederation) started showing up at the chancery, seeking to initiate dialogue and find a way to work together with the church.

A meeting took place in the chancery coffee lounge. As a result of it, Bishop Romero put Neto and me in charge of working with the CUTS in the training of workers in the unions and in the base communities. We were to teach some classes in the union's labor school. The confederation would invite its members to discussions and retreats that we would organize, and we would carry out a systematic union training program in the base communities. And so we started. Our pastoral mission among the workers must have been "discovered" by the government: it was later included in official accusations against us.

Other workers came to the chancery office with requests. They usually asked for mediation in labor conflicts. The offices of the chancery were also used from time to time as a safe place for owner-worker dialogue.

A deep understanding of the labor movement required something more than simply getting to know a few workers and mediating a few conflicts, of course, but those activities were a symbol of how the labor movement began to gain confidence in our bishop. Difficulties and fears remained, and suspicions that he might let them down. But he began to understand better a world that was new to him in many ways.

Bishop Romero's unfamiliarity with the lives and ways of working people prompted Neto Barrera to consult with us once about whether it would be a good idea to take the bishop with him to the seminars organized by the new union coordinating committee. Would he be shocked? After Neto's death we told Bishop Romero about those fears and he let us know in no uncertain terms that that was precisely why he had wanted to enter into dialogue with the workers with whom Neto had been in association.

There were many other experiences that still remain to be told and that would give an even clearer image of this Christian man who always sought to be faithful to the world of struggle and pain because of his faith.

I remember the assassination of Miguel Solís as he left the Mass held for the great labor leader José Guillermo Rivas. We wrote a profile of Miguel, labor leader and Christian militant, in *Orientación*. We spoke there of his difficult vocation and his plans to participate in a cursillo twenty days later in the seminary of the archdiocese. Bishop Romero asked us about him time and time again, about the connection between his Christian life and his political militancy.

And he was always listening, with an enormous capacity for admiration and a desire to make sense of the mystery of God's work in human beings.

January 20, 1979—Octavio Ortiz, Martyr

It was 6:30 A.M. when the leaders of the Christian communities of San Antonio Abad came and woke us up: "They've surrounded the retreat house and we've heard rifles and bombs going off!"

The night before, a youth retreat had begun there. Octavio, Chepita, and Ana María were running it, along with a team of young persons from the base community. San Antonio was at the foot of an extinct volcano; once a little town, it had been absorbed by the growth of the city. It had an immense Christian vitality. This was due, in large measure, to the work of the Belgian priest Guillermo Denoux. The community's Christian and political commitment was so intense it had spread to other communities. This was especially true among the young, many of whom had become members of the Popular Unified Action Front (FAPU).

We headed out for the hospital where Bishop Romero lived and we found other community members already there. Nothing could be done: the retreat house was at the center of a full-scale military operation. They were even using tanks. The bishop telephoned lawyers from the chancery legal aid office, and they set to work to figure out what was going on.

They learned that some bodies had been brought to the morgue. When the lawyer returned, his face was ashen; "Octavio's body is there, his face was smashed in." Bishop Romero was stunned. Octavio was an extraordinarily good person, down-to-earth, hard working. The following are some of the positions he held—all at the same time: pastor of San Francisco parish on the outskirts of town, chaplain of the base communities of San Antonio Abad, coordinator of community pastoral work for the city of Mejicanos, member of the pastoral team for the working-class neighborhoods of San Salvador, member of the Pastoral Reflection Group's archdiocesan team, vicar of his zone, representative of all the vicariates in the pastoral council of the archdiocese, member of the governing board of the seminary, spiritual director of the seminarians—and more. He never stopped smiling and no one really knew all the work he actually did.

Everyone used Octavio's house. There were community leaders meeting there, catechism courses, persons coming to use the mimeograph machine or make contact with rural base communities. Activists from underground groups came for medical care. Catechists from rural areas came to get the medical attention they needed after being tortured in jail.

Octavio was a great friend. Everyone's indignation was expressed in the phrase "no more!" Bishop Romero felt it deeply. His sermon that day was almost poetic, but he openly accused the president of the country and called him a liar for his recent public statements in Mexico. Because Romero already had his bags packed and documents drawn up for Puebla, he assigned the response to Octavio's assassination to the priests and the base communities.

In his absence, all the priests met with representatives from the base communities, and they decided to write a joint communiqué and hold a protest march in the streets of San Salvador. On January 30, 380 priests and 600 nuns and brothers took to the streets with a huge banner reading "NO MORE!" An enormous statue of Christ was carried at the head of the demonstration. From Puebla, Bishop Romero had been in contact by phone and had given his permission. The people gathered in crowds on the sidewalks to see the priests and religious march by. We had asked that the people not join the march because of the possibility of violence on the part of the police. The demonstration was a symbol of unity—the unity that our bishop had been able to fashion around the historical movement forward of the poor, amid the persecution and all the massacres. That day even Agustín, an eighty-five-year-old priest from an Italian religious congregation, participated in the protest and the march.

Bishop Romero in Puebla

From the moment that Bishop Chávez had returned from
Puerto Rico with the news of the third Latin American Bishops'
Conference, to be held in Puebla de los Angeles, Mexico, the
archdiocese began its preparations. Our church was alive,
dynamic, struggling.

When the first preparatory text arrived, disappointment hit us
all very hard. The second text was no better. We had to do something. Because the texts were useless as guides for discussion and
reflection, the base communities started to organize an alternative. A questionnaire was drawn up touching on the main themes
confronting the church of God in Latin America, especially the
theme of evangelization. All the communities studied and discussed the questionnaire and sent in their responses. A synthesis
made by our theologians on the same issues was also put together,
and with all this material we went for a week of reflection with our
bishop.

Bishop Romero had not been chosen by El Salvador's episcopal
conference to go to Puebla, but we found out that he would attend as the representative of a Vatican organization for Latin
America.

When we learned whom the episcopal conference had chosen to
represent the Salvadoran church at Puebla, there was outright
indignation, but we really should not have expected anything else:
Bishop René Revelo, Bishop Pedro Aparicio, and his auxiliary,
Bishop Fredi Delgado. The base communities published a short
life sketch of each of them, and stated that they would in no way
feel represented by them at Puebla.

And so, chosen by Rome and with the mantle of the martyrs of
El Salvador—the blood of his people and of his priests—Bishop
Romero went to Puebla with a twofold mission: to achieve solidarity for the Salvadoran people with the church in other countries, and to get them to recognize that the Salvadoran church was
under martyrdom and persecution.

In Mexico City he was accosted by reporters. He refuted the lies
of the president of El Salvador, General Carlos Humberto Ro-

mero. Our bishop spoke clearly and convincingly. He became a focus of attention for the worldwide press.

In Puebla the work was exhausting. Salvadorans were physically and spiritually there with him. The mothers of El Salvador's "missing" and the mothers of political prisoners were present; they demonstrated in front of the building where the bishops were meeting and they considered Romero "their bishop." Also present were militants of the FAPU (Popular Unified Action Front) who had just been exiled after taking refuge in the Mexican embassy; they asked to see him. The most recently expelled priest from El Salvador arrived there, as also the Salvadoran theologians who had just met with fourteen experts in liberation theology in Washington, D.C. And *we* were there, the group of priests who helped him spread information among the bishops and reporters, arranged interviews, helped him evaluate the events of the day. . . and helped him relax.

Outside the conference hall, Romero was news and was received with tremendous affection. Each time a news conference for him was announced, none of the available places could accommodate the crowd. And he always made sure that we were there.

Within the conference, he was treated with hostility and silence. Bishop Leonidas Proaño and Hélder Câmara, and a few others, were the only ones to support him. The Salvadoran bishops who were there waged war with him, and, when a letter pledging solidarity with Romero and his people was circulated, there were many conspicuous gaps on the signature list.

Every free minute he had, he met with us to tell us what had been going on and to ask our advice. But we realized that the bishops' conference was essentially closed to the Salvadoran church's experiences and hopes.

After the conference, base communities from all over Mexico wanted to have a meeting in Mexico City with the church of El Salvador.

At that meeting, in the midst of more than seven hundred delegates, Jon Sobrino talked about the theology that was emerging from our communities' life experiences. Astor, José, Luis, and others spoke of the pastoral work in our martyred and persecuted communities and of the tasks that had to be addressed by the church. Everyone there listened to Romero with enthusiasm and admiration. At the end, during the offertory of the closing Mass, they brought clothing for Salvadoran refugees and collected fifteen thousand pesos. And there were many offers of jobs and housing.

That was how the bishop's stay in Puebla and Mexico City went. He liked the description that someone gave of the bishops' conference: "The game was a tie, the score was nothing to nothing, but it was a moral victory for the people's church, because we played on an unfamiliar field and the crowd (of bishops) was against us."

"Whatever political issue we take up we must look at it in terms of the people . . . the poor."

"The poor are the body of Christ today. Through them he lives on in history."

IV

Crisis and Popular Mobilization

Throughout 1979 the economic crisis became ever more acute. Along with the economic crisis there was a corresponding political debacle which was evident in the increasingly desperate solutions that were proposed. Every so-called solution that was tried out and then failed led directly to a tightening of the screws and a new round of increasingly intense repression against the people. Reformism and repression characterized the year 1979.

The popular movement was like a giant wave swiftly growing larger and larger as it rolled in, gathering together the people in the revolutionary mass organizations. The most important single event that year was the strike at La Constancia, the beer and soft-drink bottling company. The strike was led by the José Guillermo Rivas union, which belonged to the CCS (*Consejo Coordinador de Sindicatos,* Labor Union Coordinating Council). The Meza Ayau family, owner of La Constancia, is one of the fourteen families of the Salvadoran oligarchy.

Workers seized the building and had to protect its perimeter in armed confrontations with the forces of repression. Several of them were killed. The army had the building completely surrounded. Then the first signs of solidarity with other unions began to appear. The electrical workers' union, led by the FAPU, paralyzed the country for twenty-three hours by shutting off the nation's source of electricity.

Revitalization within the revolutionary union movement threw the fraudulent model of industrialization into a state of crisis.

58

Based on El Salvador's high population density and poverty, the country had been chosen as a place to build factories by many industrialists interested in taking advantage of the need for work and the hunger of the Salvadoran people. They managed to turn the country into a kind of free zone for transnational companies. The government guaranteed low salaries and no labor unions. In response to the popular movement, those industries began to claim they were in a state of crisis. They began to close their factories, leaving thousands of workers unemployed.

As a result, May 1, International Workers' Day, could have been explosive that year, and General Romero's government tried to suppress public activities. The repression was aimed at the mass organizations. Shortly before May 1 they arrested and roughed up six union leaders including Facundo Guardado, a *campesino* from Arcatao, one of the first organizers of cooperatives and a founder of the Landworkers' Union (UTC). Later he was secretary general of the BPR and he continued to be an active participant in the Salvadoran struggle.

That was the backdrop of what we call "Heroic May," a militant popular demonstration on May Day that involved the people's takeover of churches and embassies and massacres by the military in the cathedral plaza and in the vicinity of the Venezuelan embassy. ("They fled up the steps of the cathedral as their blood trickled down.") Forty-eight persons from the popular movement were dead. We were able to rescue three leaders from the clutches of the tyrants, but three others "disappeared," and we had to assume they were dead.

International solidarity with El Salvador heightened, but we also realized we would get no help from governments such as those in Costa Rica and Venezuela. And we knew there was an urgent need for more internal solidarity among all the people's organizations.

At the same time the relationship between the popular movement and certain sectors of the church began to loosen. A group of Christian intellectuals, frustrated old-line leaders of the Social Christian Party, were out grabbing government positions in the "new democratization" or "restricted democracy." To maintain credibility with the power structure they had to criticize the people's organizations, and they did so from a falsely prophetic stance, accusing the organizations of being too secular. The intellectuals, instead of acting as a leaven for the kingdom to come, decided to become "detached" and "objective" referees of the situation. And that was why we started to hear harsh statements against our bishop: "In the end, he is going to fail us." Although he had frequently been chosen before to mediate labor problems, now, even when he offered to do so, he was rejected.

June 1979—Nicaragua Explodes

The final insurrection in June that led to the Sandinista triumph in Nicaragua sounded the bell of freedom in the very heart of imperialism. The impossible *is* possible and the empire was shown to have feet of clay. Hope was reborn among the poor of El Salvador. The people's movements had to figure out how to accept into their ranks the many more persons who wanted to become part of the revolutionary process.

The house of cards called a "new democratic opening" started to come tumbling down, along with "national dialogue" and the attempts at a "popular forum" built around the Social Christian Party. The attempt to get the people to support the traditional political parties was not working. Moreover, there would be a motion to condemn the government of General Romero at the next Organization of American States meeting to be held in October.

June 20, 1979—Rafael Palacios, Martyr

Toward the end of the 1960s, Father Rafael Palacios began his liberating evangelical ministry in Tecoluca, in the diocese of San Vicente. Conflict with his bishop was not long in coming. Bishop Aparicio, even when he appeared to be denouncing an evil, was usually maneuvering to increase his own power. Some of his undertakings were among the saddest reflections on our Christian community.

Rafael was forced to leave the diocese and was taken into the parish of El Calvario in Santa Tecla, a city of a hundred churches and a thousand traditions. But his pastoral dynamism would cause him trouble there too. Members of his local community, born of the city's poor, worked out an interpretation of Jesus' imprisonment based on their own lives of exploitation. On Holy Thursday, 1979, they acted it out in a passion play in the parish of El Calvario. The old accusations surfaced again and Rafael was criticized by some of his fellow priests and some members of the hierarchy.

He was a hard worker, poor, very quiet, and built like a prize fighter. He spoke right to the point. Despite the accusations, he kept on working as before, but now with the poorest of the poor, those who lived in and around the markets, and those who had been evicted from their miserable dwellings. He refused to be tied down by territorial or liturgical restrictions. His goal was to create communities of free Christians, there where they lived, suffered, resisted, and struggled for liberation. And the other priests became more resentful, more critical.

When Bishop Romero first came to the archdiocese the ecclesiastical bureaucrats were causing Rafael trouble because of all this. Rutilio Grande went to speak to the new bishop and told him, "Rafael is a great priest. Don't pay attention to the criticisms. Go and talk with his Christian community and you will find out that wherever he is, the gospel is alive."

This was how the friendship between Bishop Romero and the Christian community of Santa Tecla began. Many times he went to their meetings, to help with their problems. That was why one night he called together the priests who were speaking badly of Rafael and made them accuse him to his face so that they would be unmasked and have to stop. This happened at one of the priests' retreats that they both attended.

Many times, due to the number of vacancies that could not be filled in the parishes because of the assassinations and deportations of priests, the bishop wanted to place Rafael in a canonical parish ministry. But Rafael had a clear vision that the world of the poor did not revolve around parish churches and he refused. The time came, however, when he could refuse no longer and he took charge of Octavio Ortiz's parish in the city of Mejicanos.

And that was when death by assassination caught up with him. He was pastor of San Francisco, coordinator of the base communities in Santa Tecla and in the suburbs of Santa Lucía, and representative of the Pastoral Reflection Group to the National Committee of Christian Communities.

We had warned him to be careful. His work in Santa Tecla drew a great deal of attention. Besides, People's Liberation Forces (FPL) were increasing their guerrilla activity against those responsible for the recent massacres of the people, and the military had again started to take reprisals against the church. One day Rafael's car had UGB painted on it, the initials of the criminal "White Hand" (*Unión Guerrera Blanca,* White Warrior Union), another extreme right-wing organization fronting for the military. And this time they singled out Rafael. But he still did not take the necessary precautions.

On June 20, on his way back from a community meeting, they murdered him; his body fell on the streets of Santa Tecla.

Again a huge demonstration. Again Christian communities, hundreds of priests in albs and stoles, and Bishop Romero marched behind the body of an assassinated priest and friend.

The priests who had not tried to understand Rafael when he was alive, now felt guilty. Those who had made accusations against him and plagued him were now rejected by the Christian communities. But Bishop Romero had been different. He had taken Rafael under his wing, accompanied him, defended him, loved him.

August 4, 1979—Alirio Napoleón Macías, Martyr

"Napo" was a skinny, nervous, active man who always seemed to be smiling, one of the first to join the Pastoral Reflection Group. Three of his qualities were especially impressive:

• A compulsion to help the poor obtain justice. The entire parish of San Esteban was organized into base communities. Many parishioners were catechists or lay ministers. Many of them were active in the UTC (*Unión de Trabajadores del Campo,* Landworkers' Union). Napo was always bursting with plans for classes and seminars on everything from cooperatives to public health, and he somehow managed to find the money to finance his projects.

• A great affection for his fellow priests. He was always the one who held the group together and was aware of everyone's needs. He always offered to be the spokesperson to go and speak with the bishop of his diocese, Bishop Aparicio, in the frequent conflicts that we had with him. Whenever he arrived at a meeting he brightened the gloom with his smile and the joy that he always brought with him.

But I saw him cry once, too. It was when he and the nine other progressive priests from the diocese of San Vicente were suspended from their priestly duties by Bishop Aparicio for having signed a letter, along with three hundred other pastoral workers. The letter was about the papal nuncio, denouncing his anti-gospel attitudes. Napo fought to keep the ten priests of San Vicente united, but there were times when it was very painful. Their plan was not to leave their posts even though they would obey the suspension, and then to contest it together by challenging Bishop Aparicio's action in Rome. Their unity, however, was almost at the breaking point, especially because the National Guard visited them one by one. First there were threats and then two of the group were tortured. The guardsmen told them they did not have a chance now that their bishop had washed his hands of them and they were fair game.

The day that justice was done, when the suspension was lifted, we went with the base communities of San Salvador to the Mass where they were reinstated. I noticed that a number of the group of ten disappeared before lunch. Napo and I went looking for them, and we found them, so all ten were united again. After so many struggles they had wanted to share their joy, so they had gotten together in a little room in Napo's small house. And that was the time I saw him cry. . . from happiness.

• Dedication to study. He was not given to complicated scholarship, but he always arrived at our meetings with some mimeographed article, which he proceeded to hand out to us.

The *campesinos* knew that his life was in danger and they were very careful to watch over him. But on that fourth day of August, assassins broke through the peasants' defenses, murdered him, and left his bloodied corpse next to the altar, the communal table of sacrifice. The commander of the National Guard had sent a letter to Bishop Aparicio asking for information about Alirio Napoleón; a copy of this letter and Bishop Aparicio's response arrived at Napoleón's parish a few days after his death.

Bishop Romero was affected by the murder as if it had happened in his own diocese. He went to the funeral at the head of a delegation of hundreds of members of San Salvador's base communities. Bishop Aparicio was out of the country at the time and could not attend. In his stead Cubillas and Fredi Delgado arrived there, but the local people turned their backs on them, acclaiming Bishop Romero and Bishop Rivera y Damas instead.

There were thousands more in El Salvador who, after conflicts with their own bishops, felt that Bishop Romero was the center of their communion with the church.

I remember that in the month of May 1979, in San José, Costa Rica, Chilean theologian Pablo Richard asked him, "Why can't you be the bishop of all of us who are exiled from our own churches in Latin America?" We also felt this in Puebla where many saw Romero as the bishop of the people's church in all of Latin America.

August 1979—Fourth Pastoral Letter

Sharpening of the class struggle threatened to block all possibilities of a "democratic" solution to the crisis. In Nicaragua the "new society" had been born only after the suffering of insurrection. And the United States was looking for "acceptable" solutions in the Central American and Caribbean area. So it played the game of "doves" and "hawks," first laying down the card of reform and then the card of repression.

Bishop Romero's fourth pastoral letter was an attempt to keep alive the dialogue begun in his third letter a year earlier. It attempted to make understandable the Puebla document, from the 1979 Latin American Episcopal Conference, in terms of El Salvador's present situation. Again the base communities and the theologians had had their input. Some interesting points were the following:

• Many were still scandalized by rifts in the church's hierarchy. Bishop Romero, our teacher, told us that true unity was not something artificial or superstructural. Rather it was something that takes shape gradually through contact with the historical march forward of the poor. Division among the bishops was nothing more than a reflection of the divisions inherent in any class society.

• To those who claimed that they could stay neutral, our bishop repeated one of the answers to his request for input from the communities. It had been made by a priest who said, "Changes will come with or without the church but, by its very nature, the church should be part of those changes that herald the way to the kingdom of God."

• There was a maturation in the treatment of violence. Now the only violence condemned was that which "intentionally kills innocent persons or is disproportionate in the short or long term to the positive effect that is intended." Of course the letter focused on institutional violence and condemned it as the origin of the other forms of violence.

• Regarding the subject of Marxism, Bishop Romero pointed out its dangers, but stated clearly that it is a scientific analysis of economics and society, and must be analyzed from that perspective. Equally important, it is a political strategy for the people to take over power. He repeated that only a metaphysical materialistic Marxism was incompatible with the life of faith.

• Many of us were moved by the new treatment of pastoral theology. He discussed the pastoral approach to the religion of the people, the religion practiced by the basc communities. For the first time he dealt with the subject of "pastoral presence":

> I understand by "pastoral presence" the personal evangelization of those Christian individuals or groups who have made a concrete political choice, which, according to their consciences, they believe to be the historical commitment required by their faith.

Priests who were living through the politicization of our communities in general, and of our most dedicated laypersons in particular, had been demanding the legitimization of this kind of pastoral work for some time. Even though we understood all the risks that this approach implied and all the questioning of church structures that it sparked, we knew that it had to be done.

Sometimes we talked about the pastoral frontier, or pastoral discipleship, or the mission of pastoral presence. What all of those terms meant was an evangelization of presence and ferment within the people's organizations and being willing to take on all the risks implicit in it. It was part of the creation of a new culture, announcing to us what the future would be like. It was also a matter of celebrating the faith and making it explicit at the very heart of the liberation struggle, while recognizing that it has its own values and symbolism. At last our bishop understood the long years of slow work by trial and error, of discovery and fidelity.

The People Rebuffed Again

Ever since the Sandinista triumph in Nicaragua, peaceful solutions to the crisis in El Salvador seemed further and further away. Plans began to be formulated detailing the steps that would have to be taken to put the people in power. There was no chance that the "experiment in democracy" involving General Romero and the middle-class opposition would succeed.

September 11, 1979

Viron Vaky, Undersecretary for Interamerican Affairs in the Carter administration, and frequent visitor to El Salvador and the chancery, presented to the State Department a plan called "Central America at the Crossroads." In it he stated that "polarization in El Salvador is very advanced and the possibilities of avoiding violence are quickly disappearing."

He proposed a solution: "By our cooperation and appropriate aid, give support to genuine and serious reforms."

September 14

Hodding Carter, White House spokesman, said that "William Bowdler and Viron Vaky had suggested to General Romero the possibility of his resigning from the presidency as a convincing, though somewhat dramatic, demonstration of his desire for democracy in the country."

October 10

President Carter ordered a military alert for the entire Caribbean and Central American area on the pretense that there were some three thousand Soviet troops in Cuba. Senator Stone explained the U.S. military presence: "It is to increase the guaranteed effective aid of the Carter administration to countries such as Honduras, Guatemala, and El Salvador."

October 11

General Romero unexpectedly visited the United States "for reasons of health."

October 14

General Romero's family moved to the United States. That same night, in Washington, there was a special meeting of the Commission on El Salvador: Carter, Vance, Brown, and Brzezinski were present.

October 15

General Romero and his toadies, calmly and with an air of resignation, left for the United States in CONDECA (Central American Mutual Defense Organization) airplanes supplied by the government of Guatemala.

An in-house coup had been engineered by "young officers." They even invited several persons who were friends of the archbishop of San Salvador to form part of the counterrevolutionary junta!

October 16

Hodding Carter defined the new junta in the following words: "It is moderate, centrist . . . encouraging to our State Department."

The Juntas and the Crisis in the Salvadoran Church

The first junta presented itself as revolutionary and close to Bishop Romero. It was rumored that some of its members consulted with our bishop before accepting. Junta members needed the bishop because the church was the only social base that they had any chance of gaining. As someone said, the members of the junta were "Christians without a cross and without a constituency." And they offered our bishop everything imaginable.

One of the priests who was very close to the junta interviewed the bishop on the radio. The interview was transmitted simultaneously by all the radio stations in the country. Bishop Romero acknowledged that the junta members were basically honest, had a clean record, and were his friends. He asked for a grace period for them, to see if their actions would live up to their words.

Our base communities were distressed. The junta had begun repressing not only insurrectional outbursts but even the strikes that were taking place at that time. And once again the people's blood flowed in the streets—more blood than in the worst of times under General Romero.

Our bishop tried to be understanding. He said the problem was that the junta did not yet control all sectors of the government. He kept trusting in the promises of his friends and the young officers. Some priests, who felt that they were the protagonists of a new liberal government, surrounded our bishop and kept his hopes alive. We had been trying to talk with him but it was practically impossible.

A meeting was called. At it priests and laypeople of the base communities present reflected on what was happening. They decided to send a "Letter to the Communities" encouraging them to discuss the political situation and take a stand on it. They criticized some sectors of the church and of the Catholic university (UCA), and mentioned some facts to help in the decision-making process. At the end of the document some general demands were laid down, along with some more specific ones coming from the experience of the communities issuing the letter. A study guide was included, made up of questions for discussion. It was sent out to all the base communities, the parishes, and other interested parties.

Many communities felt betrayed by Bishop Romero. One, for example, refused to continue receiving the archdiocesan newspaper *Orientación*.

In mid-November the conflict came out into the open. One faction took advantage of a meeting of the Pastoral Council to make accusations against the authors of the "Letter to the Communities." They were accused of being unfaithful to the church, undermining unity, and lacking in communion with Bishop Romero. Even our bishop felt offended, and a meeting was planned to study the situation. It was set for November 28, the anniversary of Neto Barrera's death. Before the meeting, another letter was sent out by the lay representatives on the Pastoral Council. They supported the priests who had taken responsibility for the letter.

Nothing was resolved at the meeting because the positions taken were poisoned by political interests, both covert and overt.

December 23, 1979

Xavier, acting as the representative of the priests accused of being traitors to the church, had a personal meeting with our bishop. The junta had already shown its inability to control the civil oligarchy and the military tyranny. The air was cleared and a dialogue was re-established with the base communities.

January 3, 1980

Bishop Romero met with the Pastoral Reflection Group in the Domus Mariae retreat house. Again he was alone and without intermediaries, as in the old days. We began to analyze our concerns. Things were cleared up. We all practiced self-criticism.

We were now a smaller group. Those missing were either dead or deported by the military. We recalled the direction that pastoral work had taken and we discussed the accusations against us, which were either totally false or made from a false point of view:

At the beginning of our work, the Christian base communities were barely crawling. They were trying out new methods and there were many crises. . . . Then the political organizations suddenly appeared on the scene and tried to recruit community members *en masse.* The base communities are able to awaken the people . . . conscientize . . . but they do not have the means to put into practice what they realize is demanded by their commitment to love. . . .

There are many Christians who take on revolutionary political commitments and abandon the public profession of their Christian faith. One organization even puts its members in the false position of having to choose between the church and the organization. A dogmatic approach to the revolution is sometimes taught and metaphysical materialism is preached.

The need has arisen for a pastoral presence among the political organizations and for a continuing education in the faith. The search is on for a Christian identity compatible with the revolutionary process, and little by little it is being found. We have to put up with the criticism of the church that comes from the people's struggle and discover how to use it creatively.

We left the meeting reconciled, and once again Bishop Romero took a chance on us. Two conclusions had been reached: (1) we must organize meetings, study weeks, and planning sessions, and (2) the bishop and some of us should begin a direct dialogue with the revolutionary organizations—no intermediaries.

That very night a meeting was set up between Bishop Romero and the national directorate of the Popular Revolutionary Bloc (BPR). Later there would be periodic meetings with the Mass Revolutionary Coordinating Committee (CRM, *Coordinadora Revolucionaria de Masas),* according to the needs and circumstances of the moment.

The Second Junta

The massive political involvement of the people had exposed the evil of imposed reforms. But imperialism had another card up its sleeve: the old Christian Democratic Party offered to implement a new model of domination, and the struggle continued.

But Bishop Romero had acquired a base in reality from which to view the truth and he judged events from that perspective:

> Whatever political issue we take up we must look at in terms of the people, . . . of the poor. Depending on how things go for them, the church will give specific support to one political program or another. . . . The events of this week prove that neither the junta nor the Christian Democrats are governing this country. . . . The real power is in the hands of the most repressive sector of the armed forces. If the junta members do not wish to be accomplices in these abuses of power and outright criminal behavior, they should publicly announce the names of those responsible and apply the necessary sanctions, for their hands are red with blood . . . now, more than ever before. . . .
>
> The present government totally lacks popular support and is kept in power only by the armed forces and the support of foreign powers. The Christian Democratic presence in the junta functions only to disguise the repressive character of the present regime, especially outside the country.

The monthly clergy meeting in Domus Mariae, 1978

"*If God accepts the sacrifice of my life, my hope is that my blood will be like a seed of liberty and a sign that our hopes will soon become a reality.*"

V

The Path to Calvary

Meetings continued with the priests, the Christian communities, and the Mass Revolutionary Coordinating Committee. At the University of Louvain, Belgium, our bishop received an honorary doctorate. He received this kind of recognition a number of times. He always wondered if responding to public awards really benefited the people or not. When he was nominated as a candidate for the Nobel Peace Prize, he said that it was something like being in the Miss Universe contest, but that if it gave some kind of protection to the people he would go through with it. He knew that he had to speak in strong terms, because the truth was not getting out. He made his speech at Louvain perfectly clear. It was February 2, 1980:

> I am a shepherd who, with his people, has begun to learn a beautiful and difficult truth: our Christian faith requires that we submerge ourselves in this world.
>
> The course taken by the church has always had political repercussions. The problem is how to direct that influence so that it will be in accordance with the faith.
>
> The world that the church must serve is the world of the poor, and the poor are the ones who decide what it means for the church to really live in the world.

He made it clear that the church does not have a political program of its own, but rather that its role is to keep alive the hope that the people have in their own historical march forward:

The hope that the church fosters is a call . . . to the poor, the vast majority, that they take responsibility for their own future, that they conscientize themselves, that they organize; . . . the call is one of support for their just causes and demands.

It is the poor who force us to understand what is really taking place. . . . The persecution of the church is a result of defending the poor. Our persecution is nothing more nor less than sharing in the destiny of the poor.

The poor are the body of Christ today. Through them he lives on in history.

He expanded on the situation of the poor in El Salvador with words that came close to poetry:

The church has committed itself to the world of the poor. . . . The words of the prophets of Israel still hold true for us: there are those who would sell a just man for money, and a poor man for a pair of sandals. There are those who fill their houses with violence, fill their houses with what they have stolen. There are those who crush the poor . . . while lying on beds of the most exquisite marble. There are those who take over house after house, field after field, until they own the whole territory and are the only ones in it.

What hurt Bishop Romero most was to see the intrinsic evil of the economic system, which revealed its deadly consequences most clearly in dependent countries such as El Salvador. On one occasion when the cathedral was surrounded by soldiers, he preached once again, "How evil this system must be to pit the poor against the poor; the peasant in army uniform against the worker peasant." But he was even more anguished to see the faith being manipulated to serve the goals of oppression. In an interview given to *Prensa Latina* at that time, he said, "The situation of injustice is so bad that the faith itself has been perverted; the faith is being used to defend the financial interests of the oligarchy."

This was the reason for his urgent pleas to the Christians involved in the revolutionary organizations that they maintain their Christian identity within the struggle and that they find a way to make it explicit:

> Those who are involved in the process of liberation in our country can be assured that the church will continue to accompany them—with the authentic voice of the gospel.
> Christians who belong to ecclesial base communities . . . the church challenges you to reach out to a goal that will be politically valid. Christians, in this difficult hour, our country needs liberators who are morally good and a liberation that is socially authentic.

Preparing to Die

During the final days of February 1980, we celebrated the annual priests' retreat. All of the priests from the archdiocese participated in this week of reflection and spiritual encounter. That year it had special meaning. Like Jesus at the last supper, Bishop Romero felt the walls closing in on him. After the retreat he said in an interview with the Mexican newspaper *Excelsior:*

> My life has been threatened many times. I have to confess that, as a Christian, I don't believe in death without resurrection. If they kill me, *I will rise again in the Salvadoran people.* I'm not boasting, or saying this out of pride, but rather as humbly as I can.
> As a shepherd, I am obliged by divine law to give my life for those I love, for the entire Salvadoran people, including those Salvadorans who threaten to assassinate me. If they should go so far as to carry out their threats, I want you to know that I now offer my blood to God for justice and the resurrection of El Salvador.
> Martyrdom is a grace of God that I do not feel worthy of. But if God accepts the sacrifice of my life, my hope is that my blood will be like a seed of liberty and a sign that our hopes will soon become a reality.

My death will be for the liberation of my people and a testimony of hope for the future.

A bishop will die, but the church of God, which is the people, will never perish.

It is in the light of his personal beliefs, his commitment to and solidarity with the poor, and his dialogue with the Mass Revolutionary Coordinating Committee—representing the poor—that we should understand the clarity with which Bishop Romero identified the people's enemies. Our bishop felt his death coming closer day by day. On February 18 a bomb had destroyed the YSAX offices, the radio station of the archdiocese, the "stronghold of truth" as he called it that very day. Then on March 9, a suitcase filled with dynamite had been placed in the church where he was to celebrate Mass for Mario Zamora, another assassination victim.

At Louvain he had already said, "I have warned the oligarchy time and again to open their hands, give away their fancy rings, because if they don't, the time will come when they will be cut off."

In the famous interview with *Prensa Latina* he was much more explicit:

The cause of the evil here is the oligarchy, a small nucleus of families who don't care about the hunger of the people. . . . To maintain and increase their margin of profits, they repress the people.

The assassinated priests—martyrs of the God of the poor, martyrs of the poor of God—helped him see the truth clearly:

Those exemplary priests deserve great admiration. . . . They were victims of the effort to maintain an unjust system. . . . Neto Barrera, Rutilio Grande, Alfonso Navarro, Octavio Ortiz, and the others had great insight; they grasped reality with great clarity and saw that the common enemy of our people is the oligarchy.

February 17, 1980—Letter to President Carter

"Your Excellency,
President of the United States of America,
Mr. Jimmy Carter

"Mr. President:

"In recent days a news item has appeared in the national press that causes me great concern. According to the newspapers, your government is studying the possibility of supporting, by economic and military aid, the junta that is presently governing El Salvador.

"Because you are a Christian and have spoken of your desire to defend human rights, I should like to express my pastoral point of view regarding what I have read and make a concrete request.

"I am very worried by the news that the United States is studying a way of encouraging El Salvador's arms race by sending military equipment and advisors to 'train three Salvadoran batallions in logistics, communications, and intelligence.' If this newspaper report is correct, your government's contribution, instead of favoring the cause of justice and peace in El Salvador, will surely increase injustice here and sharpen the repression that has been unleashed against the people's organizations fighting to defend their most fundamental human rights.

"The present junta government, and especially the army and security forces, unfortunately have not shown themselves capable of solving the country's problems, either by political moves or by creating adequate structures. In general they have only resorted to repressive violence, amassing a total of dead and wounded far higher than in the previous military regimes, whose systematic violation of human rights was denounced by the Interamerican Human Rights Commission.

"Recently, members of the security forces dragged out and killed persons who had occupied the Christian Democratic Party headquarters. Neither the junta nor the party had authorized any such steps to be taken. This is proof enough that neither the junta nor the Christian Democrats govern the country. Political power is in the hands of the armed forces. They use their power unscrupulously. They know only how to repress the people and defend the interests of the Salvadoran oligarchy.

"Is it true that last November 'six Americans were in El Salvador . . . supplying $200,000 worth of gasmasks and bulletproof vests, and giving classes on riot control'? You must be informed that since then the security forces, with their increased personal protection and efficiency, have been repressing the people even more violently. They do not hesitate to use their weapons and they shoot to kill.

"As a Salvadoran and as archbishop of San Salvador, I have the obligation of seeing to it that faith and justice reign in my country. Therefore, assuming you truly want to defend human rights, I ask that you do two things:

• Prohibit all military assistance to the Salvadoran government.

• Guarantee that your government will not intervene, directly or indirectly, by means of military, economic, diplomatic, or other pressures, to influence the direction of the destiny of the Salvadoran people.

"We are living through a serious economic and political crisis in our country at this time, but it is beyond doubt that increasingly it is the people itself that is becoming conscientized and organized, and thereby preparing itself to take the initiative and shoulder the responsibility for the future of El Salvador. The people's organizations are the only social force capable of resolving the crisis.

"It would be totally wrong and deplorable if the Salvadoran people were to be frustrated, repressed, or in any way impeded from deciding for itself the economic and political future of our country by intervention on the part of a foreign power. It would also violate a right defended by the church. The bishops of Latin America, in our meeting in Puebla, publicly recognized 'the legitimate right to self-determination by our peoples, which permits them to organize as they wish, set their own historical direction, and participate in a new international order' (Puebla, 505).

"I hope that your religious sentiments and your desire for the defense of human rights will move you to accept my petition and thereby avoid any intensification of bloodshed in this tormented country.

Sincerely,
Oscar A. Romero
Archbishop"

Disobedience in the Service of a Higher Law

And finally Bishop Romero made a call to civil disobedience by soldiers, the "uniformed peasants." It was a decision that put him outside the bounds of legality and outside the established order. And he knew it. But our bishop had understood a fundamental, revolutionary truth of the Christian way of life: the duty to obey God before human beings.

He had already called the people to meet despite the state of seige that prohibited it. He had buried his murdered priests in church services with no other permission than the support of the local communities. He had denounced the government, the president of the republic, and the armed forces, thereby disobeying constitutional law, which prohibits such denunciations from the pulpit.

He always spoke as a free man:

Without the support of the people no government can be effective. Much less can it be so if it tries to impose itself by the force of blood and suffering.

I want to make a special appeal to soldiers, national guardsmen, and policemen: Brothers, each one of you is one of us. We are the same people. The *campesinos* you kill are your own brothers and sisters.

When you hear the words of a man telling you to kill, remember instead the words of God, "Thou shall not kill." God's law must prevail. No soldier is obliged to obey an order contrary to the law of God. It is time that you come to your senses and obey your conscience rather than follow out a sinful command.

The church, defender of the rights of God, the law of God, and the dignity of each human being, cannot remain silent in the presence of such abominations.

We should like the government to take seriously the fact that reforms dyed by so much blood are worth nothing. In the name of God, in the name of our tormented people who have suffered so much and whose laments cry out to heaven, I beseech you, I beg you, I order you in the name of God, *stop the repression!*

Source of Hope: The People's Organizations

At the same time that he called attention to oppression and its agents, he also pointed out reasons for hope. On January 11, 1980, the formation of the Mass Revolutionary Coordinating Committee (CRM) had been announced. In his sermon Bishop Romero said:

This week we have seen the first steps toward unity among the people's organizations. A national coordinating committee has been formed and it is inviting all the progressive forces in the country to joint participation.

I am pleased that they are finally breaking away from sectarian and partisan interests and managing to find a broader unity. I will always encourage this.

In the interview with *Prensa Latina* on February 15, 1980, he repeated that the organizations are the best hope for liberation:

I believe in the mass organizations, I believe in the need for the Salvadoran people to become organized. . . . The organizations are the social force that will promote, and pursue, and be able to create an authentic society. . . . Organization is necessary to be able to struggle effectively. . . . Because I am convinced that organization is important, I am very pleased to see this new spirit of unity.

In his last sermon, on the eve of his death, he again insisted on the same point: "Of course the Coordinating Committee has its faults . . . but it will be the solution to the problem if it matures and if it is able to truly comprehend the wishes of the people."

The Right to Insurrectional Violence

As Bishop Romero's thought evolved, insurrectional violence had been one of the problems that was dealt with in his give-and-take relationship with the people. In his last two pastoral letters he had explained the right that a people has to insurrection and under what conditions. And with each passing day he saw that possibility coming closer and closer to being a concrete reality and, therefore, he insisted:

> Christians are not afraid of combat; they know how to fight, but they prefer the language of peace. However, when a dictatorship seriously violates human rights and attacks the common good of the nation, when it becomes unbearable and closes all channels of dialogue, of understanding, of rationality—when this happens, the church speaks of the legitimate right of insurrectional violence.

They Had to Kill Him

They had to do it. This completely free and holy man, this man of God at the service of the historical movement forward of the poor, was costing them more alive than dead. They coldly entered into a sort of economic cost-benefit analysis and planned his death.

Of course they would have preferred to find some other solution. They sent one person after another to talk to him. They sent North American diplomats: Todman, Devine, Vaky, Bowdler. And they promised him that certain things would be done, that there were solutions within the system.

They had recourse to Rome; "apostolic visitors" came, as well as neighboring papal nuncios on "unofficial" visits. But Bishop Romero continued making the point that the laws of God are above human laws. On Sunday, the eve of his assassination, the American ambassador was seen at Bishop Romero's Mass. And the next day the same ambassador stated, as if it were the official line, that the assassination had been the work of an expert and that it could have been done by the extreme right or the extreme left. And there *he* was in the middle, washing his hands.

They assassinated him. It was as simple as that. On March 24, 1980, at six thirty in the evening. And he rose again, as he had promised.

Prophecy and Denunciation

The Christian communities, the people of God, publicly denounced the assassins of Romero: imperialism, the rich, and the instruments they use to control the country—the Christian Democratic Party, the junta, and the military tyranny.

The same communities also denounced the complicity of the ecclesiastical hierarchs who had either abandoned or fought against Romero, and they excommunicated them from his funeral. A huge banner at the door of the cathedral prohibited entrance to the papal nuncio and to Bishops Aparicio, Alvarez, and Revelo. Never before had anyone heard of such a prophetic act. It came from the kind of church that is born from the committed faith of the people.

Of the Salvadoran hierarchy, only Bishop Rivera y Damas of Santiago de María attended the funeral.

Bishops from other countries came, to be in solidarity with our people and our church.

All the people's organizations joined the protest and repudiated the despicable assassination of Bishop Oscar Arnulfo Romero. They promised to redouble their efforts to attain the definitive liberation announced by the bishop who gave his life for that cause.

Aftermath

Bishop Romero's death caused a problem for the Vatican. Bureaucratic interests within the institutional church wanted to regain control of his diocese and turn it once again into the center of tranquility and episcopal unity that it had been before Romero became a prophet of the people's church. But they could not appoint just anyone. The people had already rejected all but one bishop. He was Bishop Arturo Rivera y Damas, and the Vatican's solution was to name him apostolic administrator of the arch-diocese of San Salvador.

The task assigned to Bishop Rivera was clear: to try to rebuild the outward unity of the church around its hierarchy and smooth out the differences among the bishops who had been divided over the words, the example, and the life of Bishop Romero.

Bishop Rivera took on the task—which meant that he started to yield ground that had been won by Bishop Romero. He tried to reconcile the irreconcilable. He kept Bishop Revelo, who had been Romero's auxiliary bishop. He signed letters that he was not totally in agreement with, but he felt he had to sign them because of his mandate. He tried to find a non-existent middle ground. He was trying to be a prophet to two opposed camps at the same time. He denounced the structural sins of the junta, made up of Christian Democrats and members of the military. But he also coolly denounced errors made by the people's organizations, instead of helping to correct them through appropriate channels and personal contact.

Bishop Rivera also began to use a false analysis of the Salvadoran socio-political makeup—the same interpretation made and promulgated by the oligarchy. That analysis was, basically, that in El Salvador there were two extremes—the military and the government—and the people were caught in the middle. In Rivera's thinking, the church, inasmuch as it should be with the people, should be like the central upright of a balance, identified with the people, with the two ends of its crossbeam representing the military and the government.

That was during the first months after Bishop Romero's death—but the junta systematically continued its massacre of the people. Bishop Rivera began to see that he would have to change his position. He had to be faithful to the people. By September 1980 he accepted the analysis that had been adopted by Bishop Romero, and he took up Romero's prophetic stance. He began to explain the real situation in El Salvador in terms of the confrontation of a people with the tyranny fomented by the military and the government—instigated and manipulated by the oligarchy.

The public denunciations by Bishop Rivera, his return to a truly prophetic stance, unleashed the forces of repression against the church once again. And the repression escalated. First there were the bombs that destroyed the bishop's chancery office, the dynamite that silenced the "stronghold of truth," YSAX, two bombs in the Jesuit house, and the bombing of the residence of the Belgian priests. And the violent entry of soldiers into churches, killing more than sixty Christians who were there to call attention to the repression of the people by the government.

Then the death of a Christian leader, Magdalena, in charge of the Human Rights Commission, the break-ins at several parishes in the north of the country where the communion hosts were profaned, and the soldiers demonstrated even more their rage and irrationality. They defecated inside the churches in order to show their contempt. After many other threats were made, they capped it all with the killing of yet another priest, Manuel Reyes.

October 7, 1980—Manuel Reyes, Martyr

Manuel had been a chaplain in the Salvadoran air force. He devoted much of his time to study, because he felt he was still young and should develop all aspects of his personality. Politically, he was somewhere between a reformer and a revolutionary. He began to find himself on the side of the people through his work in one of the most classic neighborhoods of San Salvador—"CIOS" *(Colonia 10 de Septiembre)*. But events were rapidly leading him toward a commitment to the organizations of the poor who were already on the road to liberation.

In order that the news of Manuel's assassination would not get around too fast, his assassins blew up YSAX, the archdiocesan radio station, before they killed him. However, the people found out and they celebrated the liturgy of his funeral in such a way that it became a cry of rebellion.

On October 7, 1980, his body had been found on the road leading to the town of Mariona, where political prisoners were incarcerated. The church was once again where it should always have been: in the midst of the people—and surrounded by wolves.

CONIP

The unity of the church in and around the historical movement forward of the poor found expression in the founding of CONIP

(Coordinadora Nacional de la Iglesia Popular, National Coordinating Committee of the People's Church). The Salvadoran church born of the people's faith had evolved rapidly since 1970 and had formed several unifying organizations. When Bishop Romero became the archbishop of San Salvador there was already an organization called the National Council of Peasant Christian Communities. During the period of his service to the church of San Salvador the Coordinating Committee for Urban Christian Communities came into existence. Through participation in the struggles of the people, unity between those two organizations grew and in August 1980 they formed CONIP. It took up the work left unfinished by Romero and made it possible for the church to become ever more deeply committed to the struggle of our people, and to become an example for the church in all of Latin America.

"Saint Romero of the Americas"

Despite silence on the part of the institutional church and the Latin American Episcopal Conference, and their nonrecognition of Bishop Romero as someone important in the history of the Latin American church, he is by no means forgotten. The people know how to identify the people of God in their history, and throughout Latin America the image of Bishop Romero is recalled, eulogized, and kept alive. Songs and poems dedicated to him are flourishing; a beautiful anthology could be made of them. Books are being published of his sermons, his theological contributions, his pastoral letters, his example. His life is being studied in a search for something very valuable: the key to keeping the church at the heart of the people's struggle.

And solidarity grows. Christian groups in solidarity with the Salvadoran people's struggle emerge throughout all of Latin America—and beyond—and name themselves after Bishop Romero.

Within El Salvador, where the people are preparing for a definitive liberation battle, Bishop Romero's dream is becoming a reality—the unity of all the poor so that they can create a society of justice and equality. The people have forged a unity in the Farabundo Martí Front for National Liberation. Five million individuals trying to become a people are a people of God on pilgrimage.

And we see clearly the truth of the words of Bishop Pedro Ca-saldáliga of São Felix, Brazil, in a poem that he dedicated to the memory of Archbishop Romero: "Saint Romero of the Americas, no one will ever silence your last sermon."

Fr. Rutilio Grande, S.J.,
assassinated March 12, 1977

Fr. Alfonso Navarro,
assassinated May 11, 1977

Fr. Rafael Palacios,
assassinated June 20, 1979

Fr. Alirio Napoleón Macías,
assassinated Aug. 4, 1979

Fr. Manuel Reyes,
assassinated Oct. 7, 1980

Appendix

We, the bishops whose signatures follow, have come from diverse parts of the world to pay Christian homage to Bishop Oscar Arnulfo Romero, the shepherd of his people, the faithful witness of Christ, defender of justice and the poor.

For defending the life of his people and striving for a society of justice and peace, he was murdered, like Christ, at the moment of offertory. We have come here, representing our churches and our peoples, to protest this horrendous crime, and to celebrate with the Salvadoran people and church the new life that his martyrdom will invigorate.

Many of us knew Bishop Romero personally. We saw in him the example of the bishop we dreamed of in Medellín and Puebla. Bishop Romero was a deeply religious man and a faithful follower of Christ: a man of prayer, of sincere humility, of pure heart and deep love for his brothers and sisters. He put his human and Christian vision of life at the service of his pastoral office. The difficult situation at the time he became archbishop of San Salvador made him mature and grow even more in his devoted following of Christ. From the very beginning of his ministry, he had to witness the blood of martyrdom and the suffering of his people. That blood and that pain strengthened him in his determination to be the faithful and understanding shepherd who never abandoned his flock, who lent them his voice, and who gave his life for them.

In Oscar Romero's ministry as a bishop there were three things that we especially admire and for which we are especially grateful.

In the first place, he was a preacher of the faith and a teacher of the truth. He never failed to speak the truth, and to speak it with evangelical courage, because he believed that God's truth enlightens the hearts of individuals and penetrates to the truth of society. He was faithful to the church and in close communion with the vicar of Christ. He tirelessly announced the good news of Jesus Christ, his message, his teaching. He tried very hard to transmit the life of Christ to his flock so that they, as the offspring of God, would meet and have respect for one another in fellowship. He never shirked his obligations as a teacher. Even at the risk of his life, he always spoke the truth about the situation of oppression and repression to which the poor are subjected. He searched for ways to clarify conflicts through faith, through study of the demands and hopes of his people, and especially through his life of prayer with the Lord.

In the second place, he was a vigorous defender of justice. Like the ancient prophets, and like Jesus, he denounced evil-doers and lashed out at those who were willing to "sell the poor for a pair of sandals," who stole the fruits of their labor, repressed them and then murdered them when they fought for their lives and their rights. And, like the prophets, he always dreamed of, worked toward, and struggled for a true society of brothers and sisters, so that the kingdom of God promised by Christ would become a reality.

In the third place, he was a friend, a brother, a defender of the poor and oppressed; a friend of the *campesinos,* of the workers, of all those who were forced to live in misery. His deep faith in God and his total commitment to Christ motivated him to see Christ in them and to defend the cause of the poor as being the cause of God himself. If Bishop Romero was partial to anyone, it was to the poor and oppressed. This was clearly shown in his love for them and his defense of them. From that stance, from his solidarity with their lives and their struggle for integral liberation, he taught a love that was true and a peace that was authentic. That was where he put his faith, because in social injustice and the threats against the life of the poor he saw the most radical atheism; whereas in the life of the poor, in the efforts they themselves were making to change their life of misery, he saw the dawning of the glory of God.

Bishop Romero was an exemplary bishop because he was a bishop of the poor on a continent cruelly disfigured by the poverty of the vast majority of its inhabitants. He joined them, defended their cause, and shared their fate: persecution and martyrdom. Bishop Romero is a symbol of a whole church, a symbol of the whole Latin American continent, Yahweh's true suffering servant burdened with the sins of injustice and death on our continent.

Since we feared he might be assassinated, we were not surprised by it. His fate could not have been any other: he was faithful to Christ and had truly incarnated himself in the suffering of our people. We know that Bishop Romero's death is not an isolated incident. It is part of the testimony of a church that in Medellín and Puebla made the evangelical option to side with the poor and oppressed. Because of the martyrdom of Bishop Romero we now have a deeper insight into the meaning of death— death from starvation, death from disease—the death that permeates the lives of our people. We also better understand the uncountable martyrdoms, the innumerable crosses we see marking the path that our continent is following at this time. They have crucified *campesinos,* indigents, workers, students, priests, pastoral workers, nuns. Bishops are imprisoned, tortured, and assassinated for believing in Jesus Christ and for loving the poor. As with the death of Jesus, these atrocities are the result of human injustice and yet, at the same time, they are also the seeds of resurrection.

As we look at the corpse of Bishop Romero and so many others who have been assassinated, we want to repeat our condemnation of and our protest against this insanity. We are pleading, as did Bishop Romero in his last sermon, for an end to repression everywhere—on the entire continent, and especially in this beloved and tormented country, El Salvador. We pray to God that the faith of the Salvadoran people be strong and that he send them a new shepherd to follow the same path. That is also the petition of the hundreds of thousands of faithful who are here with us today. Finally, as bishops, we commit ourselves and our churches to follow the path of Bishop Romero. We intend to complete his sacrifice of the Mass, unfinished because it was interrupted by the bullets of his assassins.

Bishop Oscar Arnulfo Romero is a martyr of the liberation called for in the gospel, a living example of the shepherd proposed as a model in Puebla. To him, to the poor of the continent, and to our Lord Jesus, we direct our petition for the grace to be more faithful in our commitment to the poor and oppressed, the chosen people of God, and to be ever more resolute in the struggle for justice and in being faithful witnesses of God and his kingdom.

San Salvador, March 29, 1980

Archbishop Marcos McGrath, Panama
Bishop Luciano Mendes de Almeida, Brazil
Bishop Leonidas Proaño, Ecuador
Bishop Sergio Méndez Arceo, Mexico
Bishop Gerardo Flores, Guatemala
Bishop Eamon Casey, Ireland
Bishop Luis Bambaren, Peru
Bishop Alberto Iniesta, Spain
Bishop Oscar García Urizar, Guatemala
Bishop James O'Brien, England
Bishop Arturo Rivera y Damas, El Salvador
Bishop Mario Ruiz, Ecuador
Bishop Jaime Brufau Macía, Honduras

COMMUNIQUÉ OF THE PRIESTS, NUNS, AND BROTHERS OF THE ARCHDIOCESE OF SAN SALVADOR

After having proclaimed the coming of the kingdom of God for three years as archbishop of San Salvador, Oscar Romero, standing before the altar of God, on Monday, March 24, 1980, at 6:25 P.M., was assassinated. He was killed by those who reject peace based on truth and justice. He died at the altar, precisely at the moment when he was preparing to offer the bread and wine that would become the Body and Blood of Christ. After having preached that a life offered up for others is a sure pledge of resurrection and victory, his life was taken. His martyr's death crowns his life as prophet, shepherd, and father of the Salvadoran people, especially of those most in need.

The brief ministry of Bishop Romero in the archdiocese of San Salvador had the same characteristics as the ministry of his Master and Lord in the land of Judea. The bishop was above all a follower of Jesus, of the Jesus who proclaimed the kingdom of God, who preached words of hope and of love, took the side of the oppressed, and tirelessly denounced injustice and repression. He was a follower of the Jesus who was open to all who searched for reconciliation in justice, and who was accused of being a blasphemer, a disrupter of public order, a rabble-rouser. Like his Master, Romero was assassinated by those who hate the truth and repudiate the thought of a basic fellowship and equality among the children of God.

Bishop Romero was able to unify the entire archdiocese around his person. First he gathered the poor and dispossessed. Until they heard it from his pulpit, the poor had never clearly understood that the church should have, and does have, a preferential commitment to them, and that this commitment is alive and means something in practice. The words of his sermons were welcomed with love and hope by the thousands of oppressed and needy all over El Salvador.

He united around his person the clergy, both diocesan and religious. In spite of the difficult times, never before had priests, brothers, and nuns been so united among themselves or so unified in their pastoral work. Bishop Romero himself said in his sermon on that last Sunday that the pastoral achievements of the archdiocese were not due to him alone, but to the entire archdiocese in faithful pursuit of the teachings of Medellín and Puebla. He encouraged all who were searching for real social change, which would do away with injustice, oppression, and repression.

Because of all this, and without really wanting it, Bishop Romero became a national hero. At the international level he became the most famous and respected Salvadoran national of his time. Through it all, he gave himself to everyone and asked nothing in return, spending himself and exhausting himself for the liberation of all.

The press, radio, and television of the whole world broadcast his word and the message of his commitment. Thanks to him, the word of God, the word of the Salvadoran people, the cries of the people of God, were heard throughout the world. His voice became so widespread and so penetrating that the enemies of peace decided they would tolerate it no longer. And they went to kill him in front of Christ's altar, while he preached peace, while he was offering the bread and wine that did not become the Body and Blood of Christ, because his task, though ended, was unfinished. The passion is still incomplete and the final resurrection is far in the distance, because there is so much to do before the second coming of Christ.

In this sense Bishop Romero is not dead. In El Salvador the many hearts that are still alive, the love of justice and the hatred of injustice, belie his burial. He planted so much and in such good earth that the seed will yield a hundredfold. The Salvadoran people must know that Bishop Romero still lives, that the clergy of the archdiocese follow in his path and commit themselves to making sure that his voice will not be silenced and his mission will not be interrupted. God will watch over us and see to it that his martyrdom will bear magnificent fruit for the church and for the people.

We pray to our Lord God for this to come about, and we ask Pope John Paul II to send us a new shepherd who is as similar as possible to Bishop Romero. This is what the people of God want, this is what the priests want, this is what the brothers and nuns want, this is what the archdiocese needs. God our Father knows this; he read the heart of Bishop Romero and he understands the needs of his people.

God our Father blessed the archdiocese by sending this profoundly religious man to be with us for three years. He was a pastor to the core. He knew how to apply the teachings of Vatican II, Medellín, and Puebla, and how to be faithful to them. His involvement in the political and social spheres was something he had to do because of the real-life context in which he lived. He neither asked for it nor went out looking for it. We ask the pope to send us a shepherd who can follow in the footsteps of the man who was our shepherd for the last three years.

The priests, brothers, and nuns of the archdiocese of San Salvador make this request because we intend to continue our commitment at this time of such difficulty for our country. We want to help in making the light of the Lord conquer the darkness, the truth of God win out over injustice, and the hope of the Spirit put an end to suffering. We also want to help in channeling the inheritance that Bishop Romero bequeathed to our country. For that reason, we demand, as he did, an immediate end to repression. We demand that human rights be truly respected. And we demand respect for the right that he fought for to the very end—the right of the poor, the *campesinos* and workers, to organize themselves without external hindrance. We ask that peace be restored to our land with the participation of all its popular and democratic energies. And we ask that other countries help us in this difficult but constructive task, not by providing weapons of death, but by providing support, understanding, and the protection of life.

Sorrowful and grieving, but full of faith, love, and a hope that does not let us turn back, we urge the people to continue forward. God will not let you down. Do not let your sorrow discourage you, or your anger confound you.

In memory of our friend, father, and shepherd, we have unanimously decided to declare eight days of mourning for the solemn celebration of his martyrdom and for strengthening our faith. Bishop Romero will be helping us from his place in heaven, so that soon we can all sing together the glory of resurrection on a new earth that will vibrate with the energy of a regenerated humankind—Christians who know how to love God because they know how to love their neighbors.

Press Release of the Bishop Oscar Arnulfo Romero National Coordinating Committee of the People's Church

The systematic repression that has afflicted our people for years has now become utterly unbearable: oppression, exploitation, and extreme poverty have turned the people of God into a people robbed of their human dignity. These inhuman conditions have also taught the local church to question its role on this earth and to become more closely identified with the poor.

Christian communities in the countryside and in the cities are part of this people. We are motivated by the message of the gospel and by what we have learned in living out our Christian commitment. Years ago we recognized the need to unite and coordinate our efforts; up to this point it has been done in separate groups.

But the recent escalation of military repression, the lack of understanding in some segments of the clergy and hierarchy, and the lack of communication between the base communities have shown us that we need to evaluate and benefit from the shared results of our experiences.

Hence, on this day, August 3, 1980, when we are commemorating the first anniversary of the martyrdom of Father Alirio Napoleón Macías, we have formed a coordinating committee. It brings together urban base communities from San Salvador, Santa Tecla, and surrounding areas, with rural base communities from various parts of the nation. Besides laypersons, its governing body includes priests, seminarians, and nuns who are at the service of the communities and who are committed to a pastoral plan dedicated to the liberation of the poor.

We salute the enormous achievements of Bishop Romero in his service to the people of God. As a coordinating committee, we commit ourselves to accept the theological legacy he left our church and to continue his pastoral work. Because of this commitment we have taken for ourselves the name: Bishop Oscar Arnulfo Romero National Coordinating Committee of the People's Church (CONIP).

The objectives we propose for ourselves can be divided into two basic categories:

1. Renewed organization of our pastoral presence and work in the midst of the people:
   a. in their practice of religion (pastoral work with the masses)
   b. within the Christian base communities (intensification of internal pastoral work)
   c. within the people's political organizations (pastoral presence).
2. Integrated participation in the liberation of our people.

In El Salvador we see, as did Bishop Romero, only two political forces: (1) that of North American imperialism supported by the Salvadoran bourgeoisie and the junta; by "reforms" and repression it tries to perpetuate capitalist exploitation; (2) that of the exploited people; acting according to their faith they have organized themselves to create a new society and a new people, with a revolutionary, democratic government.

It is only within this framework that the present situation in El Salvador can be clearly and exactly defined. We, the Christian base communities, support and will work for the effective implementation of the people's plan for liberation from exploitation. From a biblical viewpoint, the present situation is comparable to the conflict between David and Goliath. Goliath (the powerful) is very arrogant; he shouts that he is ready to smash and destroy everything that stands in his way. David (the people, impoverished and suffering) is looking for small stones with which to confront the giant. We all know how the story ends. . . .

Our Appeals

To the Salvadoran people, to the poor of El Salvador, and to their truly representative organizations: Continue your courageous and heroic struggle for liberation from all domination and exploitation to which we, as a people, have been subjected for four centuries. We joyfully communicate to you that, as CONIP, we promise to continue the pastoral approach of Bishop Romero and we pledge our fidelity to the gospel and to you.

To the Christians of El Salvador: Search for the word of God, the fountain of life and hope, so that it may enlighten your faith and prompt it to concrete deeds of justice and love in fellowship. In this way you will become active participants in the struggle we are all carrying out to build a new society where the values of the kingdom of God can be lived and shared by all Salvadorans.

To the Christian base communities: Continue your religious work of service to the country's poor and oppressed, and from that experience extend your work to other Salvadorans of good will, so that they will commit themselves to the building of a new society for the good of all. For greater effectiveness in this work, we invite the Christian communities that are not yet with us to join the coordinating committee.

To the priests, religious, and seminarians who, following the gospel of Jesus Christ, carry out their pastoral work in the midst of the people: Join with us and work with us in the renewal of the Christian base communities in El Salvador.

To our bishops: (1) Maintain a bond of unity among us, through your commitment, your understanding, and a mutually enriching dialogue. (2) Let your word be a light that brings joy and illumination to the historical march forward of the poor, and a condemnation of the sinful efforts of the powerful. May your word provoke true conversion in the hearts of all! (3) Through your presence among us, under the guidance of the Holy Spirit, who makes all things new in history, learn how to confirm the direction that the church and the people are taking, to bring the kingdom of God closer to us.

To all the peoples of the world: Give us the solidarity that our church and our people so badly need in order to remain faithful to our evangelical mission, and to win the victory that will put an end to the death-dealing system that we are no longer willing to tolerate in El Salvador.

We hope that solidarity of this nature will become a reality through actions supporting our people's political organizations, and by rejecting the reformist and repressive plans that the powerful are trying to impose on us. We ask you to try to see in our struggle an example that will encourage you to struggle against and destroy whatever prevents human development according to God's plan.

May the hope that now gives light to our people become the hope of all peoples in the world!

Cathedral of San Salvador, August 3, 1980
Coordinating Council of CONIP

Maura Clarke,
Maryknoll missioner,
assassinated December 2, 1980

Ita Ford,
Maryknoll missioner,
assassinated December 2, 1980

Jean Donovan,
lay missioner,
assassinated December 2, 1980

Dorothy Kazel,
Ursuline missioner,
assassinated December 2, 1980

Persons interested in becoming involved with Central American solidarity groups are encouraged to contact the Washington Office on Latin America. WOLA is a church-sponsored ecumenical agency advocating human rights and social justice in Latin America.

WOLA
110 Maryland Ave., N.E.
Washington, DC 20002
Tel.: 202-544-8045